PETER KENNEDY

THE MAN WHO THREATENED ROME

'Portrait of a Rebel Priest' by Martin Flanagan
'The People Speak' by Michele Gierck

Introduction by Paul Collins

With contributions by
Frances Devlin-Glass, Michael Morwood, Hans Kung,
Brian Doyle, Sr Veronica Brady, John Shelby Spong,
Fr Roy Bourgeois, Sr Joan Chittister, Fr Peter Norden,
Tom Uren, Shane Howard and others.

one day hill
Publishers Australia

National Library of Australia Cataloguing-in-Publication entry

Author: Flanagan, Martin.
Other Authors/Contributors: Gierck, Michele.

Title: Peter Kennedy : The Man Who Threatened Rome / Martin Flanagan, Michele Gierck.

ISBN: 9780980564365 (PBK)

Subjects:
Kennedy, Peter.
St. Mary's Catholic Church (South Brisbane, Qld.)
Catholic Church--Australia--Clergy.
Catholic Church--Australia--Discipline.
Catholic Church--Doctrines.
Church renewal--Catholic Church.

Edited by Bernadette Walters
Copyedited by Ian Sibley
Set in Palatino
Printed in Australia by Griffin Press
Designed by Gail Pearce, The Wizarts

Dewey Number: 282.092

Quid hoc ad aeternitatem? – *What does it matter in the light of eternity?*

No-one knows anything about God and those who say they do are just troublemakers (Rabia of Basra, 14th-century Muslim mystic)

The most important thing is not to stop questioning (Albert Einstein)

CONTENTS

TIMELINE OF ST MARY'S, SOUTH BRISBANE

by Maggie Boyle

1858–1870

- A grant of land for 'R.C. Church purposes' at South Brisbane was applied for and approved by the NSW Dept of Land & Public Works.
- By 1866, Mass was being said in the small wooden chapel on the south side of the Brisbane River, and a school was run on weekdays by a lay teacher under the auspices of the Sisters of Mercy.

1870–1880

- The Sisters of St Joseph with their founder Mother Mary MacKillop came to Brisbane and established schools in Queensland. St Mary's at South Brisbane was offered to them as their first school and the Sisters soon established their convent in a former hotel near St Mary's in Montague Road. In 1880, all the Queensland Sisters were removed by Mother Mary MacKillop because of difficulties with Bishop James Quinn.

1880–1900

- South Brisbane grew rapidly during the 1880s, became a town and built fine buildings.
- The parish of South Brisbane was formally established in 1892 and a presbytery built to house the appointed parish priest. A new church was designed for St Mary's, and the foundation stone was laid in 1892. It opened in July 1893.

- The Sisters of Mercy took over the school and the small wooden church/school was expanded.
- The 1890s were difficult with floods, bank crashes and workers' strikes, and South Brisbane's growth was severely hampered by the main river bridge being washed away in the 1893 flood.

1900–1930
- Parish expands. A new convent school was opened in 1909. The infant school continued in the old chapel until the late 1920s and was then demolished. The Sisters of Mercy built a convent nearby in 1915, ending their daily journey from All Hallows on the north side of the river.
- St Mary's church was refurbished and a new Sanctuary added in 1929.
- Industrial development expanded along the river and railway in the inner-city region.

1930–1970
- More suburbs developed and people moved out of inner-city areas. South Brisbane was less desirable as a residential area.
- Postwar migrants moved into the area and St Mary's became the Mass Centre for four groups of migrants: Polish, Dutch, Lithuanian and Slovenian.
- Numbers at the church and school declined. The school closed in 1964. The convent closed in 1968.

1970–2000
- The last parish priest left in 1980. By that time, fewer than 50 people were regularly attending the church services. South Brisbane was deemed to be no longer a parish.
- Fr Peter Kennedy was appointed Prison Chaplain for South East Queensland and Administrator of St Mary's. He moved into the St Mary's presbytery to live in Sept 1980. He was Prison Chaplain for 6 years.
- From 1987 Fr Peter built his house in Numinbah Valley and planned a spirituality centre there. He presided at 3 weekend services at St Mary's and attendances increased each year at the church services. Few of those attending live locally; they come from all areas of and around Brisbane.

- People were challenged by Fr Peter to be more involved in St Mary's and the first 'gathering day' was held in 1989. Groups looked at how to move forward as a community and under what sort of leadership.
- An elected Leadership Team was in place by 1995. Part-time liturgy and community workers were employed by the community. Attendances at weekend liturgies numbered around 800. Focus of the community was on spirituality, hospitality and social justice.
- By 1998, Micah Projects Incorporated was well established. The Leadership Team and community worker resigned in that year. Fr Peter decided to take back control of the community and to work more closely with Micah Projects, focusing on social-justice issues. Fr Terry Fitzpatrick and Fr Peter Kennedy were financially supported by the community. A part-time liturgy worker was employed by the community.

2000–2009
- A community council was appointed.
- Focus of community was social justice and hospitality.
- Numbers attending St Mary's slowly decreased until 2004, and then gradually increased again. In 2008 there was a sharp increase in numbers.
- The liturgy had changed over the years, welcomed by many, but not by all. Changes from 2004 onwards caused some people to leave, but others to attend. In 2008 the changes were challenged by the Archdiocese.
- In February 2009 Peter Kennedy was sacked by his Archbishop for contravening aspects of Catholic doctrine.
- From the end of April 2009, Fr Peter Kennedy and all of those who support him no longer attend St Mary's. Micah Projects Ltd moved out of the parish house at the end of June. St Mary's-in-Exile is relocated to the Trades and Labour Council building, South Brisbane.
- At the beginning of October 2009, there are around 70 people who attend 2 services at St Mary's on each Sunday. The Dean of St Stephen's Cathedral is currently the Administrator of St Mary's.

INTRODUCTION:

SAINT MARY'S
COMMUNITY AND PETER KENNEDY:
PROPHETIC WITNESSES

by Paul Collins

The first time I met Peter Kennedy was in early 1974 at Sancta Sophia College at Sydney University on what was the first Marriage Encounter weekend ever held in Australia. I remember it well because Peter and another priest and I got into serious trouble with the organisers for slipping out on Saturday evening for a quiet drink at the pub across Missenden Road. When we got back rather late that night we were bluntly told by the American couple running the event that 'we were not taking things seriously enough'. Given that the husband was a tough-looking Italian-American cop from Brooklyn, New York, we expressed immediate apologies for our behaviour, even though we felt like naughty boys being rebuked by their parents. Peter was the chaplain at Nowra Naval Air Base at the time, and I was teaching church history and pastoral theology at Saint Paul's National Seminary in Sydney. Despite our misbehaviour, Marriage Encounter went on to be a great success in Australia and is still going strong.

This all happened in those optimistic days a decade after Vatican II when many Catholics, like the people running Marriage Encounter and priests like Kennedy and I, still felt that the renewal and rejuvenation of the Church was possible. Sure, there were signs that all was not well with the ecclesiastical institution, but we were young, committed and trusting enough to feel that what we were doing was what the Holy Spirit and the Church had asked of us. This was several years before the October 1978 election of John Paul II. His 26-year-long papacy was to bring our optimism to a grinding halt and did much to stop renewal in its tracks. Two decades later we all became aware of the sexual-abuse crisis. A more tragic and debilitating crisis is hard to imagine. Nowadays those of us who still call Catholicism home tend to be far more realistic about the possibility of changing clericalism or the church.

Mass-attendance figures were certainly not at the forefront of our consciousness back in 1974. However, if we had looked closely at the statistics for that year we would have found a considerable decline in the numbers of people present every week at Mass from the historically unprecedented highs of around 65% of all Catholics in 1955 and 55% in 1962, to probably somewhere around 43% to 44% in 1974. For sure, Mass attendance is only a very rough indicator of commitment, but it at least gives you some basic facts with which to work.

Things have certainly further changed in the three and a half decades since 1974. The vast majority of Catholics have pretty much given up on the Church if practice rates are any indication. Robert E. Dixon of the Australian Catholic Bishops' Conference Pastoral Projects Office in his book *The Catholic Community in Australia* (2005) shows that in 2001 15.3% of Catholics (i.e. about 765 000 people out of a total Australian population of 18.76 million) attended Mass on a typical weekend that year. Most (13.3%) of these attended every weekend. This is a 28% drop on 1974 figures. When we look more closely at these figures we see that for those aged between 25 and 34 the drop in attendance was double the overall average, with only about 6% to 7% of this age group attending Mass regularly. What is even more significant is that nowadays the drop in the number of women attending is roughly equal to that of men, whereas in the past female attendance was always higher. In our culture women are still the significant influencing factor in religious affiliation. Another important issue is that 'around 60 000 of the 775 000 people aged 15 to 24 who had identified themselves (or had been identified by their parents) as Catholics in the 1992 census did not identify themselves that way in the 2001 census, when they were aged between 25 to 34' (Robert E. Dixon et al. Research Project on Catholics Who Have Stopped Attending Mass, Final Report, ACBC, 2007, p. 4). In other words, about 60 000 young people in that period ceased to call themselves as Catholics at all, let alone attend Mass. Significantly attendance at Mass has dropped even among older Catholics in the over-60 age bracket.

After talking to researchers, bishops and priests, my own guess is that in the eight years between 2001 and 2009 a further decline has occurred. Now only about 10% of Catholics, or even less, attend Mass regularly. In raw statistical terms that would mean that about 512 000 out of a total Catholic population of 5 126 000 now attend Mass regularly. That means that more than 250 000 Catholics have stopped practising between 2001 and 2009.

In the light of all this Bob Dixon makes an illuminating comment: he says that attendance rates vary widely from parish to parish and diocese to diocese and that 'high attendance rates are often the sign of an attractive parish, one not attended only by Catholics who live in the parish but also by others who are prepared to cross parish boundaries in search of a satisfying experience of worship' (Dixon, *The Catholic Community in Australia*, p. 96). This brings us right back to Peter Kennedy and the community of Saint Mary's, South Brisbane. Back in the early 1970s South Brisbane was the pits, an industrial wasteland of wharves and derelict buildings. The turning point was the World Expo of 1988. Now South Brisbane is the trendy, up-market, inner-city dwelling place of singles and younger couples without children. This is certainly not a fertile ground for regular church-going or religion of any sort. Yet every Sunday Saint Mary's was filled to overflowing several times over. There must have been something happening to bring people there when other churches, often served by equally good, pastoral, intelligent priests, were at best half full. Certainly the priest is part of the equation, but he is not the whole picture.

Many people have said that it was the strongly participative liturgy, the highlighting of the role of women, the acceptance of all comers, and the inclusive nature of the celebration that attracted them to Saint Mary's. No doubt all these issues are part of it, but I suspect there is more to it. The strong social-justice orientation of Saint Mary's has also contributed. There would probably be no other local Catholic community in Australia – with the possible exception of Father Bob Maguire's parish of Saint Peter and Paul in South Melbourne and the Sacred Heart Mission in Melbourne's Saint Kilda – who are doing more in terms of local Christian service. Micah Projects, the social-justice arm of Saint Mary's, receives some seven million dollars of state and federal government grants for its extraordinary work which has socially transformed South Brisbane and beyond.

Peter Kennedy's personality is also part of it. There is a contemplative feel about him, as well as a simplicity and honesty which is disarming. His admission about his own uncertainty concerning basic beliefs such as the divinity of Christ or the existence of an afterlife, or whether heaven and hell are real, reflects the kind of confusion that many of us feel today. It's all very well to rattle off the Nicene Creed at Mass without reflecting on what we're really saying. But many Catholics and Christians who have thought about the creed are put off by the kind of theological language it uses, rich and meaningful as it might be to theologians. It is simply not the way many contemporary Catholics think about God, Christ, the Holy Spirit, belief and the meaning of human life. Today we think in interpersonal terms, we use the language of love and affection, and as the heirs of Freud, Jung and modern psychology it is difficult if not impossible for us to embrace the philosophical categories that created the Nicene Creed and the definitions of person and nature in the Godhead that are derived from the Council of Chalcedon (451 AD). Peter Kennedy gives voice to these kinds of reservations and in so doing encourages others to do the same. To doubt, to question and explore is what he's attempting to do. And that is why people respect him, because they are involved in the same quest. This doesn't mean that their faith is weak; it is simply that they have the strength to ask hard questions.

To accuse him of 'heresy', as some have done, is outrageous. Heresy requires at least a formal ecclesiastical process that would certainly involve the Congregation for the Doctrine of the Faith in the Vatican. As someone who has experienced this process I am in a better position to talk about it than most. No such process has ever been instituted against Kennedy. In fact, he is no more heretical than Archbishop John Bathersby. It is just that Kennedy and Bathersby approach faith differently and both their approaches enrich the fabric of Catholicism. In some ways my personal approach to faith probably has more in common with the Archbishop than it does with Peter, but I recognise and respect the fact that people come to faith and live their beliefs in different ways and with different intensities at various stages in their lives. All that Kennedy has done is to have the honesty and integrity to admit his questions, and that is precisely why he is so effective a pastor. Nowadays mature Christians don't need to be told the answers. They need the freedom to explore the questions.

I think another unspoken element in the mix is the Saint Mary's building itself. While scarcely an architectural masterpiece, it is attractive, especially inside. There is a kind of openness, even spaciousness, about it that embraces you. It feels like a real worship space. And outside it looks like it belongs on the site where it is. That is why the recognition of prior Aboriginal ownership of the land was a powerful argument that could have been more effectively used in the dispute with the archdiocese. The notion of sacred space has a real resonance in the Saint Mary's situation.

During the public phase of the crisis in 2008–2009 I also could not help noticing that a number of reporters who called me for comment confided to me off the record that they were non-practising Catholics, but when they had gone to Mass at Saint Mary's they experienced 'something' that touched them and left them with the feeling they wanted to come back. Journalists are often hard-bitten, cynical souls who are not easily 'touched' by anything, least of all religion, so I found their comments striking. In fact, it is the 'something' that you can't put your finger on, the ethos or élan of the place that holds the key to understanding the success of the community and Peter Kennedy. It is a whole lot of disparate things that somehow came together to make Saint Mary's what it is.

It is interesting to contrast the ministry of Saint Mary's community with those who have attempted to destroy it. The attack began with a small group within the Catholic community who constantly need to monitor other Catholics' beliefs, those who are now caricatured as the 'temple police'. The term comes from the New Testament where there are two references to 'temple police'. The first is in the Gospel of John (7:32, 45–6). Here Jesus is speaking in the temple on the Feast of Tabernacles when the chief priests and Pharisees 'sent temple police to arrest him' because of his messianic claims. The police were deeply impressed with Jesus' teaching and backed off arresting him. When challenged by the priests and Pharisees they replied, 'Never has a man spoken like this' (7:46). The second reference is in the Acts of the Apostles (5:12–24). Again the scene is set in the temple and this time it is Peter and the apostles who impress the people. The high priest and the Sadducees send the temple police to arrest them, but during the night they are miraculously rescued from prison by an angel, and this time the crestfallen police have to report, 'We found the prison securely locked and sentries standing at the doors, but when we opened it we found no-one inside' (Acts 5:23). The temple police were actually a distinct force that kept order within the temple itself and sometimes outside if there was a riot or disturbance. They are certainly not portrayed as bad in the New Testament; in fact they are impressed with Jesus and his apostles. So Saint Mary's reference to 'temple police' is really a gentle jibe.

But sadly gentleness is not a characteristic of the modern-day temple police. Nowadays they are a tiny remnant of a small group from the late 1990s who called themselves the 'Australian Catholics Advocacy Centre' started by a lawyer named Paul Brazier from Penrith, NSW. This outfit was always only a very tiny group numerically, but there was a particularly activist branch in Queensland. Despite its size it was this group which apparently influenced Rome to issue the infamous 'Statement of Conclusions' drawn up by a group of Vatican bureaucrats severely rebuking the Australian Bishops at the Oceania Synod in Rome in October-November 1998. The bishops were told that Catholics back home in Australia were suffering from a 'crisis of faith … manifested by the rise in the number of people with no religion and a decline in Church practice … [which was due] to Australian tolerance and openness'. The bishops were further informed that this 'can lead to indifference, to the acceptance of any opinion or activity as long as it doesn't impact adversely on other people'. Not a single one of the Vatican bureaucrats who prepared this statement was a natural English-speaker, let alone an Australian, and it's a safe bet none of them had ever visited Australia. But this didn't stop them 'knowing' precisely what was wrong with the local church.

The material upon which the statement was based seems to have been collected by members of the Australian Catholics Advocacy Group. Certainly they went around to parishes, took notes on sermons or recorded them and reported priests and bishops for any 'deviations' from what they construed to be orthodoxy. They swore statutory declarations about what they had heard and seen at parish liturgies. This material was collected centrally and sent on to Rome. At most they had the support of a couple of Australian bishops.

The temple police seem to be the kind of people who psychologically can't tolerate the fact that others may have different approaches to faith to them, or have doubts, or who may want to express their beliefs in different, less theologically precise language. Essentially they take the 'catholic' out of Catholicism and try to reduce the church to what is essentially a sect. Catholic faith is about freeing people and deepening their ability to love and serve others. Sects, in contrast, govern by rules and fear. People inclined to be sectarian are exclusivist and can't stand a faith that embraces rather than banishes, that is pastoral rather than righteous. They are the ones who, in the name of Truth (with a capital 'T'), attempt to terrorise the rest of us into submission. It was Kennedy's and Saint Mary's openness to the questions and their willingness to include rather than exclude that led the current temple police to attempt to undermine their ministry.

Here it is worth examining their methodology. When they discover 'deviations' in parishes, they report them first to the local bishop. But they are not really interested in him or his views. They just want to be able to claim to Rome that he has 'done nothing' to address their complaints. Sometimes even the bishop himself is the object of their gripe. Their real aim is to go to the Vatican with the 'evidence' of deviation that they have 'discovered'. Archbishop Bathersby himself told ABC Radio National's *Religion Report* on 24 February 1999 that 'Rome would constantly be receiving messages from people in the various churches around the world not only from what you'd call formal messages from formal sources. But . . . as well there'd be quite a lot of information filtering through by means of letters, and perhaps even direct contact from other people in the church, particularly lay people in the church.'

Bathersby is right: this is precisely what happens when a person or parish is targeted. They bombard specific officials in Rome whom they already know to be sympathetic to their notion of Catholicism with letters, and then follow that up with visits to the Vatican seeking appointments with these officials, and no doubt wining and dining them. Saint Mary's would have been characterised as a kind of soft-core, new-age commune posing as Catholic, and Kennedy as a kind of non-believing priest-heresiarch.

In the case of Saint Mary's I suspect that the specifically targeted officials were primarily in the Congregation for Divine Worship (the Vatican department which looks after liturgy), and I'd be willing to bet that the senior official involved was the then Secretary of the Congregation, Archbishop Malcolm Ranjith, a Sri Lankan who in June 2009 was appointed Archbishop of Colombo. Ranjith was the bishop behind the brief excommunication of the Sri Lankan theologian Father Tissa Balasuriya in 1997. Ranjith believes that there needs to be a 'reform of the reform'; that is, the reforms of Vatican II have gone too far and they need to be further 'reformed' along more restrictive lines. For Ranjith liturgy is the natural starting point in this process. Here he thinks we need to recover a sense of the sacred. What would have happened is that Ranjith would have talked to colleagues in other Vatican departments, particularly the Congregation for Bishops and the Congregation for the Doctrine of the Faith. All three Congregations would then have written to Bathersby putting pressure on him to solve the problem by closing down Saint Mary's and silencing Kennedy. The question of the pastoral effectiveness of Saint Mary's seemingly never arises with these Vatican officials. They are besotted with control and they get away with it unless bishops like Bathersby intervene to inform them of the effectiveness of communities like Saint Mary's and defend the local church.

Archbishop Bathersby is a good man and he has certainly been held in high regard in Brisbane and in the wider Australian church. For fifteen or more years he allowed Saint Mary's to exist and to prosper while other parishes were slowly dying. But from about 2004 onwards the pressure from the tiny remnant of temple police grew, and when the Vatican became involved Bathersby could no longer avoid the issue. Kennedy was accused of not wearing vestments at Mass, of allowing lay women to preach and of using alternative Eucharistic Prayers. Father Terry Fitzpatrick was attacked by *The Australian* (2 October 2008) for using the baptismal formula 'We baptise you in the name of the Creator, the Sustainer and the Liberator of life who is also Father, Son and Spirit'. What theological authority *The Australian* had to speak on this issue is anybody's guess. Tess Livingstone, one of the paper's Brisbane-based journalists who wrote about this issue, clearly lacked objectivity and certainly had it in for Saint Mary's. She is also the biographer of Cardinal George Pell.

By 2008 things were coming to a head and the pressure was on Bathersby. He reacted rather negatively and, in my view, could have handled the affair differently. Kennedy and Bathersby have known each other since they were boys and, as I told the ABC's *Australian Story* (25 May 2009), 'I think a couple of pretty big egos were involved. Some people have compared it to alpha males … So it's clear to me that a certain amount of ego was involved on both parts.' While I do think Peter 'upped the ante' at times, I consider that the ultimate responsibility for what happened lies with Bathersby, who lost my sympathy when he talked about calling in the police to evict the community from the church. The archdiocesan chancellor, Father Adrian Farrelly, certainly didn't help matters; at times he seemed to be pouring petrol on the fire rather than exercising restraint and trying to build some bridges. Bathersby often talked about Saint Mary's severing communion from the Brisbane archdiocese and lacking respect for him as archbishop. This seems to be a very narrow view of the nature of ecclesial communion. Bathersby himself has been deeply involved in ecumenism and part of that involves recognition of the communion that exists between the Christian churches and some recognition of their sacraments and rituals, which certainly differ from those of Catholicism. Catholics are actually able to have Communion in the literal sense with the Orthodox churches, although the Orthodox certainly has reservations about communion with us. So for the archbishop to talk so glibly about a break in communion between Saint Mary's and the archdiocese seemed to me premature. I would have looked for the tolerance, protection and the kind of understanding he has so often shown to other Christians. If we can't sort it out with our own people, how can we do it with people of other faiths?

A homily preached by Dermot Dorgan at Saint Mary's Community in Exile on 6 July 2009 expresses the central issue between Saint Mary's and the archdiocese. Dorgan, with great clarity, began his homily by defining prophecy. Prophets, he said, are 'people gifted with the ability to see deeply into the present, to look below the surface of society and see the undercurrents and hidden realities that determine what is happening or will happen. The word "seer" is a good description.' Like Jesus, prophets are certainly not well received in their own country or community.

INTRODUCTION:
SAINT MARY'S COMMUNITY AND PETER KENNEDY:
PROPHETIC WITNESSES

Dorgan points out that prophets like Martin Luther King and Archbishop Oscar Romero were killed, the Jesuit paleontologist Pierre Teilhard de Chardin was silenced by the Vatican and Mary MacKillop was excommunicated. He then listed some of the prophetic aspects of the Saint Mary's community, the precise things that annoyed the critics. And then he puts his finger on the essence of the issue: there are as many ways of talking about the experience of love and of God as there are people. And that is what Saint Mary's tired to express.

But, as Dorgan says, 'If some authority were to come along and say, "Look, all this multiplicity of words is downright confusing. From now on we're going to have one formula for expressing this experience [of God] and here it is – blah, blah, blah. From now on this is the only orthodox way of expressing this experience. All other expressions are inaccurate and invalid", well, we can see how ridiculous this is. But [as Catholics] we're tied to certain fixed expressions of the experience of God, and I believe it is a prophetic act – the act in fact of adult Christians – to look for other ways of expressing our experience. So all these things, which have caused such offence to others, can be seen as prophetic acts. And predictably, they have landed us in hot water.'

Dermot Dorgan is exactly right. The key thing is that the Australian church doesn't lose or forget the prophetic actions of Saint Mary's community and Peter Kennedy. They have so much to teach all of us.

Paul Collins is a church historian and commentator on Catholicism. He is the author of twelve books and a former specialist editor–religion for the ABC.

His most recent book is Believers – Does Australian Catholiscm Have a Future?

PORTRAIT OF A REBEL PRIEST

by Martin Flanagan

Peter Kennedy had dispensed with being called Father long before I met him. That was after morning Mass on 15 March 2009, the Third Sunday of Lent. I had attended Mass at St Mary's to hear Kennedy speak from the pulpit. He did so but only briefly. In the course of what he had to say, he declared it was the First Sunday after Lent, then corrected himself and said it was the Fourth.

At that time, Kennedy had been a priest all his working life except for a period of three months when he was a trainee accountant. Kennedy 'hated' accountancy. He was supposed to go to technical school at night. Instead, he went to a nearby cathedral. He has always had an ability to pray or, as he now terms it, to enter the realm of 'no-thought'. To go for hours without thinking. That's his strength, always has been. It got him sacked as a trainee accountant but it edged him towards the priesthood. For years, he knelt in churches, meditating on the tabernacle and the host that devout Catholics believe becomes the body of Christ through Mass.

Although Catholic church is integral to his story, I told Kennedy before we met that I was more interested in knowing about him than his dispute with the church. The arguments surrounding his actions, both for and against, are, to my mind, obvious. I wanted to know what I always want to know when I interview someone. Who are you? And why are you? He received the request much as if it were another of life's puzzles that he would need to contemplate. When we started the interview, I had a faintly unnerving feeling that comes occasionally to people in my trade when you realise you are with someone who may just – literally – answer any question you ask. I don't sense he fears the personal inquiry.

His story, as I heard it, went like this. He is the product of an unhappy marriage. His father was a large character: an optimist, a drinker, a gambler, an Irish Catholic – the sort, he says, who said the rosary on the way to the racetrack to help his horse win.

His first memory is being given a new teddy bear. He would have been, he supposes, about 18 months old. In the memory, he's standing in his crib. He's given a new teddy bear. He throws it away – he wants his old one.

His second memory – he would have been three or four – is of his mother crying. His father has been drinking. The child says to his father, 'I hate you and I will always hate you. I love her.' He says he ended up on good terms with his father but for many years the barrier to their relationship was the father's drinking and his behaviour when drunk. He tells me of another memory he has from around age 11. He is standing outside his parents' bedroom, beating on the door. He can hear his mother weeping. He is crying out: 'Leave her alone! Leave her alone!' That was also why, as a boy, he loved that moment when the family knelt at the end of each day to say the Rosary. That was a time of peace.

He didn't like school. They made him do subjects like maths and chemistry. He wanted to do subjects like art and carpentry. At fifteen, he tried to talk his father into letting him leave school. His father's firm views on education came not only from the fact he was a teacher – he was also the son of an illiterate Irishwoman with a deeply held conviction about formal education. Kennedy says his father and two elder brothers decided to send him to boarding school at St Joseph's College in Brisbane to toughen him up.

As anyone who has been to an all-male boarding school knows, sport is the passport to social acceptance. He wasn't good at it. He always wore spectacles until recent years when an operation successfully cut the cataracts from his eyes, which means that at odd moments they capture the light. 'About eight' boys from his final year at school joined the seminary. When he told his father he was thinking of joining them, his father said, 'It will mean you can never be married.' He laughed out loud at the memory when he told me that. After what he'd seen, why would he want to be married? He actually inserts a swear word in telling me the story although he adds, 'I wouldn't have sworn then.' He does swear, not a lot, but to get a sense of Peter Kennedy you need to understand that he can, and does, use strong language.

His life sounds lonely. His father was a warm, embracing man. His mother wasn't like that. He sees now he is more like his mother in type. In speaking of other people, I note that he often reduces them to types, relying on a system called enneagrams which presumes humans can be reduced to nine personality types. When we met, he had been 44 years a priest. For seven years, he was assigned to the Navy – or, as he puts it, in the Navy. These were his loneliest years, but, even on a battleship, he could still find peace by creating a small space in which to pray and say Mass. At night, he would sometimes kneel on the deck and look up at the heavens. That, he says, was quite something.

But the Navy, inadvertently, delivered a crucial freedom to the priest who was by now in his thirties. As a young man, he had what are called 'scruples'. His conscience could not be stilled. Having gone once to confession, he would feel the need to go again. The Navy cured him of that. There was no confessor at sea. He had to learn to get by on his own resources. With the money he received for his service in the Navy, he spent a year at a Jesuit centre for spiritual reflection in the United States. He doesn't remember having an epiphany, a moment when his beliefs began to change. The change, he says, was gradual.

Judging by his conversation, the most vivid of his priestly experiences were in Queensland prisons over a six-year period starting in 1980. I note that in telling stories about things that he saw and heard in prison he called the warders 'screws' – as prisoners do. In one story, a 'screw' bawled out a prisoner who wanted to debate a sermon Kennedy had just given on forgiveness. The prisoner said to the guard, 'I'm talking to Father Kennedy.' The guard said, 'I don't give a fuck who you're talking to.' Telling me this story, he cried, sharp jets of emotion down both sides of his face. 'I didn't have the guts to stand up to him,' he said. During the three hours I was talking with him, I saw emotion of this intensity half a dozen times.

Mostly, though, he was smiling – nothing beatific, more a sort of tough amusement. At seventy-one, he was still muscular although not a big man. He reminded me of those monks who are physically proficient, who chop the wood and carry water while contemplating Zen riddles about the sound of one hand clapping. Before I left, he loaded me with books by writers not known to me. Basically, their message was that any sort of personal story is a fiction and the price we pay for indulging such fictions is a loss of human awareness. That meant the possibility of excommunication held no fears for him whatsoever. He realised Hell was a figment of the imagination years ago.

I attended Mass twice at St Mary's on the Third Sunday of Lent in 2009. Something I noticed was the powerful place of women in what is called the liturgy. They gave the Mass its early shape and direction. The ones I heard speak had commanding presences and, in that sense, were good at what they did. There were vigorous readings from the Easter Gospels – a drama in which a leader of a group of social outcasts finds himself in opposition to the religious authorities of the day. The obvious parallel with Kennedy's situation was unstated but nonetheless apparent to me and, it seemed, others.

Both Masses began with Aboriginal activist Sam Watson performing the Aboriginal ceremony known as Welcome to Country. St Mary's has a treaty with the local Aboriginal people, the Jagara. The church, a basilica in the Italian manner which dates to the 1880s, has a collection of old religious statues of the sort that were standard in Catholic churches in Australia fifty years ago with Jesus, Mary and Joseph looking like pious northern Europeans with white skin, apple cheeks, blue eyes and soft brown hair. Interspersed with them are four paintings by Aboriginal artist Jarnarra Goering Goering placing St Mary's in an Aboriginal map of the area. The area around St Mary's, centring on Musgrave Park, is a traditional Aboriginal meeting place for people from many different parts of Queensland.

Kennedy did not appear in the morning service until near the end. He spoke in a strong voice, telling the congregation of the latest development in his dispute with the Archbishop, John Bathersby. Kennedy had been advised of the Archbishop's team for a forthcoming mediation. The Archbishop's team included one, and possibly two, male clerics who were canon lawyers. In response, Kennedy announced St Mary's team – five women and a Murri (the Queensland word for Koori).

At evening Mass, he didn't even give the sermon. That was given by Jeff Halper, an Israeli Jew who heads a committee seeking to re-build Palestinian houses destroyed by the Israeli military. 'People like us tend to feel powerless and marginalised,' said Halper from the pulpit. 'What you learn travelling the world is that we are the people.' Halper said there is what he calls 'an international civil society.' At the end of the service, I saw him wearing a sticker which said 'I love Saint Mary's.'

The first Mass-goers I spoke to at St Mary's were an elderly Brisbane couple, Catholics, proudly wearing 'St Mary's Matters' T-shirts. After that, I encountered an agnostic, an elderly couple from the Uniting Church and a man who may have been mentally unwell and was talking about chaining himself to the church in the event of an eviction. The last person I spoke to, an elderly woman helping with the clean-up, was Protestant. St Mary's has been her church for 15 years. She was suspicious of me, this man with a pad asking questions. The belief at St Mary's, corroborated by press reports, is that a spy from an ultra-orthodox Catholic group visited their church, then lodged a complaint with the Vatican. As a result, there were doctrinal matters upon which Peter Kennedy was accused of having erred – for example, denying the Virgin birth. 'I've never said that from the pulpit,' he said. 'But can I not discuss the issue?' He had also blessed homosexual unions and varied the formula for baptisms prescribed by the Vatican.

Basically, Peter Kennedy refused to submit to the authority of the Roman Catholic Church. In fact, he declared that he took his model for his church from the historical period before the Roman Emperor Constantine got involved. Kennedy sees that part of church history as being the moment when Christianity met power politics. 'He used Christianity to unite his Empire,' he said. Kennedy likened his church to the one that met in the catacombs, persecuted by the Roman authorities.

St Mary's the day I attended was full of people who looked like ordinary church-goers – there were just a lot more of them than there are in most Catholic churches around Australia. As a church, it had a spirit of quick and active compassion. The evening I went, it found $1500 for Palestinian housing. Kennedy told me of a notorious pedophile that the Queensland government was unable to house upon his release from jail because of community action groups and inflammatory stories in the local media. The man, ostensibly free and still in need of a place to live, was the ultimate outsider. In the end, the government turned to the St Mary's community to assist them.

I asked Kennedy if he had ever turned anyone away from his church. Only one, he said. That was a man who started taking photographs during a baptism. Believing him to be one of those sending complaints to the Vatican, Kennedy went over and knocked the camera from his hand. 'I said, Get out!' When I met Kennedy the first time, there was muted talk of occupying the church, although I sensed reservation for the idea when I discussed it with an official at Micah, St Mary's social welfare arm. The archdiocese had responded with the threat of a lockdown. He asked me what I thought that would mean. 'It could mean people who enter the site are arrested,' I said. 'Then I'll go to jail,' he replied.

Martin Flanagan is a poet, storyteller, author, journalist and public speaker. As a journalist and writer he has interviewed George Best, Sir Edward 'Weary' Dunlop, Barry Humphries, Rajmohan Gandhi, Ron Barassi, Peter Cook, Patrick Dodson, Archie Roach, Paul Keating, Don Watson and singer Paul Kelly. He has had meetings with the Dalai Lama and Queen Elizabeth II.

THE
PEOPLE SPEAK

by Michele Gierck

MICHELE GIERCK

Chance meetings are like invitations. They can take you into lives and places you would not otherwise visit. Two such meetings led to significant journeys in my own life. The first was meeting a Salvadoran refugee in an inner-city pub in Melbourne, in 1989. This encounter became my first step on a long, arduous, yet life-changing journey to El Salvador. This was at a time when human-rights abuses were rife and civil war racked this tiny Central American nation. The second chance encounter was meeting an Australian woman from Brisbane at a bus stop in a backstreet of Sydney. She had worked as a nurse in Ethiopia and Cambodia. In the course of our conversation, and a subsequent chat over a cup of tea, she offered me an open invitation to visit St Mary's in South Brisbane. That was in 2003.

The two events are linked. In many ways the former prepared me for the latter. Although Irish-Catholic culture was part of my family inheritance, had I not lived in El Salvador I doubt I would have been a person who attempted to live with faith, to enter into the mystery. And had I not lived and worked among the ecclesial base communities in El Salvador, communities for whom poverty, war, human-rights abuses, drought or floods had taken a toll, I would not have experienced what marginalisation does to people and communities. How it robs them. These experiences have become part of who I am. They inform the way I view and engage in the world.

In 2004, at 45 years of age, my adventures in El Salvador were well past. Life had changed dramatically. A back injury which had begun in 1999 persisted. Life as I had known it – working, swimming, driving, and going to the football – was constantly curtailed. Bouts of improvement were soon overridden by setbacks. And the setbacks were riddled with fatigue and pain. It seemed there was only one option left. Treatment at The Back Stability Clinic at the Mater Hospital in Brisbane. That's where I headed.

With my focus on surviving the plane trip and getting to my first appointment at the clinic, securing accommodation had been secondary. A place to stay for the first week had been arranged. Somewhere else to stay would surely work out. That was the hope.

But four days into the trip, walking down Boundary Street in West End, I began to worry. Reading the advertisements in the local real-estate agent's window did little to quell rising angst. Prices for week-long temporary accommodation were more than my budget for six weeks. In a city in which I knew few people, had to pay medical bills and live on a small budget, my sense of being alone in the world escalated.

That was when I remembered the woman at the bus stop. And St Mary's. When I rang the church, I was put through to Fr Terry Fitzpatrick. He was happy to meet with me the following day. On my way there, I stopped at the bakery on Boundary Street to buy some cupcakes for our morning tea, then pounded along the footpath up Merivale Street. The sun was casting a shadow over the garden at St Mary's that backs onto the street. I walked up the driveway. A few men from the homeless men's hostel next door to the church were seated on the church driveway. I noticed one. Bare-chested, the soft purple satin pants he wore contrasted with his hardened, weathered face. Venturing along the verandah of the old church house, I passed a few in need who were milling about. Inside there was a buzz of activity. Several people rushed past reception. I waited inside.

In person Fitzpatrick was as affable as he had been on the telephone. He showed me into his small office, pulled up a chair and we began to chat. He was warm, welcoming and humorous. We even fought over which of us would get the cupcake with the pink icing. If my memory is accurate, we halved it. He may be heavily involved in social-justice projects, but unlike many of the social activists I've met, he also has a deeply meditative side.

It was over a cup of tea that I launched into my two requests. I explained that I had written regularly for Australian Catholics and *Eureka Street* magazine, and I had been commissioned to write a few features for the Queensland newspaper, *The Courier-Mail*. Might he know of any refugee people I could interview? Secondly, and of a more urgent nature, I needed a place to stay. Only two nights separated me from temporary homelessness.

Before I left, Fitzpatrick asked me to wait in a communal area. There was someone he wanted me to meet. Waiting there, I found myself in the company of an Aboriginal artist, a Murri woman. We started to chat. She showed me some of her paintings. They were rich vivid oils, so enticing to the eye. They became more exceptional when you listened to the accompanying stories. Some of her paintings hung inside the church. In the course of that conversation I commented on how welcome I'd been made; how Fitzpatrick felt he could find me a place to stay. She showed no surprise. She thought that was normal. 'Here at St Mary's,' she said, 'no-one is ever turned away.'

Next morning at 7.45 a.m., I received a phone call. It was Gwenneth Roberts from St Mary's. 'We'd love to have you,' she said. I was shocked, delighted, relieved. Next day Gwenneth and her husband John drove over to collect me. Although I didn't know it, this stay would be the first of many.

Within days, I was attending my first Mass at St Mary's. In spite of not being able to sit down, I stood at a side entrance on a mat. The tiny car park filled up quickly. The fellow selling *The Big Issue* stood in front of the main entrance. Many greeted him by name and asked how he was. Inside, music was being rehearsed, and readings were being prepared.

What I recall about the first few services at St Mary's was the number of people who sat not in pews, but on the floor; the way people who were new to the church were introduced or welcomed and the freedom of people to come forward with their prayers or news. Also memorable was the way a slice of a tree trunk which had become the altar stood regally in the centre of the church; how Mass is said in the round, that is, with people facing each other, singing to each other, declaring what they believe to each other. Here people participated in the same liturgy that is said in so many Roman Catholic churches around the world, yet it seemed much more alive. It was communal, deeply spiritual, and so related to daily life. What's more, it felt like the most natural place for me to be.

Once my treatment at the Mater Hospital was completed and my articles written, I returned to Melbourne. But the thought that I had been welcomed into a family and a community stayed with me. I returned when I could.

In 2006, I was back in Brisbane. Not for treatment. This time I was launching my book, *700 Days in El Salvador*. While the Melbourne launch was in a bookshop, the Brisbane launch was at St Mary's. Ahead of the event, I'd sent a copy of the book to Fitzpatrick. When I arrived in Brisbane, Fr Peter Kennedy let me know he'd read the book too. It wasn't a cursory read. He'd read it carefully, and he liked it. He recognised that I'd been in some tough places. I appreciated this acknowledgement. I was invited to give the homily. There is a power, perhaps grace, in telling your story to people who listen, who welcome and accept you.

My next visit to Brisbane was for six weeks in December 2006. While there, Sunday Mass and Monday night meditation became part of my weekly rhythm. Two days before Christmas a friend I hadn't known long arrived. On Christmas Eve, I mentioned that I wanted to go to Mass. He could visit West End – close to St Mary's – or come along. To my surprise, he opted for the latter.

My friend went to Catholic schools, daydreaming his way through so many religion classes and Masses that his knowledge of Catholic culture is minimal. One legacy, however, of his Catholic upbringing is guilt. He is well acquainted with it. The last few times he had been to church were for weddings, one of them being his own, and funerals, one of them being his wife's.

When we arrived, St Mary's was packed. Even staking out a place by the side door was difficult. The priests, Kennedy and Fitzpatrick, casually dressed, were just two more faces in the crowd until part way through the celebration. To my surprise my friend sang along with the songs he knew. During the service there was a baptism. It took him a while to realise that the couple whose child was being baptised were women. At the end of the service, after I introduced him to Fitzpatrick, I asked my friend what he thought. He hadn't minded the service at all. His only comment was that things had changed since he last went to Mass, the implication being that it had changed for the better.

There has been considerable turmoil between St Mary's and the Archbishop of Brisbane. As I write this piece, the community of St Mary's is now in exile. It seems to be a long, sorry tale, one which I have watched from a thousand kilometres away. One thing I learnt through my experiences of war and postwar reconciliation is that issues are rarely black and white. There's always murky grey.

Tales of fracture, schism or silencing are not uncommon in the Catholic Church. But I would like to tell one story of reconciliation. It is a tale that so many people who participated in it told me. It is about a community and an archbishop.

The scene is El Salvador, in a poor part of the capital called Zacamil. Six hundred people died in that neighbourhood during the civil war. This story, however, begins in 1972, soon after the military occupation of the National University, before the war officially began. The Catholic bishops had issued a statement supporting the government line. This had incensed the ecclesial base communities. They wanted to speak to Monsignor Romero, then auxiliary bishop, so they invited him to Zacamil to concelebrate Mass with three other priests. He accepted.

What the congregation had not expected, however, was the homily he delivered. It was so critical of them being political rather than Christian that midway through Mass, one of the priests took off his alb, saying this was not the condition in which Mass could be celebrated. When their priest left, the congregation followed. The Mass was never finished. Only a few stayed to argue with Romero. The community was in shock. They wondered how the church they felt such a part of could be so cut off from the people, from the poor.

Years later, when Romero was Archbishop of San Salvador, he came back to the same people in the same church at Zacamil. His first words were to ask for forgiveness for what he had said to them at that Mass years ago. He also reassured them that he was determined to accompany his flock. Not one of the people who were there that day will ever forget his humility, or the commitment he made, not only to the congregation gathered but to many other communities like theirs. It was a commitment that cost him his life.

It is important that we tell our stories. That we have time for reflection. And inspiration. St Mary's has been an important part of my journey. Just as I wrote about people in the ecclesial base communities in El Salvador, so I accepted the commission to write about people from the community of St Mary's. I also offered the Archbishop of Brisbane an interview. When I met with him, he was open and amenable, and even invited me back. However, his office advised prior to our meeting that the Archbishop would prefer 'not to be involved with the book on St Mary's'. I was glad to have met him and to have made the offer. I felt I could do no less.

KARYN WALSH

There is a saying in Africa that it takes a village to raise a child. If the Australian equivalent of the village is a community, then Karyn Walsh has lived this adage.

Karyn recalls living with her sister, Vicki, in St Patrick's Boarding School in Mackay. It was a temporary measure. Her mother had planned it that way. But those plans soon changed when the girls' mother was killed in a car accident.

At the time, Karyn was nine and Vicki was six. In such a case children might be expected to be taken care of by their father. But that was out of the question. He was in hospital in Brisbane with tuberculosis, hundreds of kilometres away.

Karyn is not emotional as she tells the story. She simply relates it as a formative aspect of her life. Besides, around 40 years separate the woman she is now from the child she was then.

With the children's best interests in mind, it was decided to keep them in the boarding school. They would visit their father and extended family during school holidays. When their father recuperated, he went back to construction work building roads and bridges in northern and central Queensland. He came to see his daughters when commuting to Mackay was possible. But he was often a man on the move. His address changed with each new project.

Some of the children's relatives were not happy with the girls remaining at St Patrick's boarding school. Not because they would not be well looked after. What worried them was that they might become Catholics.

'My parents didn't practise anything. Dad's mum was Catholic, so too her sisters, but she married a Scottish protestant and thought she was going to hell because she was outside the Catholic Church.' Other close relatives belonged to the Anglican Church or the Uniting Church.

The boarding school, however, soon became their home and the two young girls became Catholic. The way Karyn describes it, it wasn't so much an upbringing as an environment. An intensely Catholic one. 'Everything around us was Catholic. Each morning at Mass there were the Pykes with their large family who lived up the road, the boarders and the nuns. We all sat in the same seats . . . our chores were often in the chapel, and there were bells to get up in the morning and to go to bed.' She laughs at the memory. It's a hearty laugh.

Yet Karyn soon discovered opportunities to have some fun. Her school was on a river, a place she visited regularly. The river became her special place. Here, unlike at boarding school, she managed to avoid trouble.

Karyn and Vicki also enjoyed going to the home of boarders on the weekends, most of whom lived on sugar-cane plantations. Those families may not have been well off but they embraced the sisters. Karyn reflects on her life at boarding school and the weekend visits. 'I got a sense of community from that. We were raised by a community really. I learnt that life is interconnected with people other than your family.'

The girls also began to spend longer holidays with their father's aunt and her family, who were strict practising Catholics and lived behind the church at Booval, Ipswich. Although she was only nine when her mother died, Karyn says faith was something that she hung on to. 'I had a feeling that it was deeper than all the superficial stuff.' She found comfort in going to church and in seeing the candles. She liked to go to St Patrick's church at night because it had an air of something special.

By her teenage years, Karyn had developed inner strength and a pragmatic approach to life. She also learnt that the Gospels could be related to the world around her. That impressed her. Karyn's faith since adolescence has been grounded in practical expression. Every Saturday for eight years she went to the same old woman's house and mopped her kitchen floor. She didn't have to do it.

It may well have been an escape from boredom, but through it she learnt something she felt was important, something she still believes. 'Small things done consistently can make an enormous difference to people. It doesn't always have to be big things.'

While a student she immersed herself in the Young Christian Students group. It was an exciting time reading the Gospels rather than relying just on church documents; looking at the surrounding environment and asking questions, encouraging critical thinking, then taking action.

After secondary school, Karyn began nursing training at the Mater Hospital in Rockhampton. On completion of her nursing studies, rather than work in a hospital she chose to go into youth work in the Rockhampton diocese. She also spent 18 months in the novitiate with the Sisters of Mercy. But the tension between religious and lay life became too much, so Karyn left.

By the time she moved to Brisbane, Karyn had several years of experience working with young homeless people. When she met Peter Walsh, who was doing similar youth outreach work in inner-city Brisbane, it seemed like a perfect match. They married two years later. Karyn became part of a new family. But within three years she lost her sister. Vicki to Leukemia. She was 26 when she died.

Karyn and Peter Walsh had not envisioned a traditional way of life. At a time when youth unemployment and homelessness were rising, and there wasn't an established social-service system in Queensland for youth homelessness, the couple felt compelled to act. After much voluntary work, they secured a grant and set up an old convent as accommodation for the homeless. There they lived with the young people they sought to assist. They also advised government.

At that same time, Fr Peter Kennedy, who was a prison chaplain and who also became the parish administrator at St Mary's, was thinking about what needed to be done in the local community. The three knew each other well. St Mary's was the parish Karyn first went to when she arrived in Brisbane. Peter Walsh had met Kennedy when he was working with homeless youth and the friendship between the two men flourished. Kennedy was also the priest who celebrated Karyn and Peter Walsh's wedding.

Karyn says that Kennedy was always passionate about the 'Option for the Poor' and liberation theology. But he was also very honest about how difficult it was for him to get inside the shoes of another person, to really understand why, for example, they ended up in prison; what their life was like. Doing that also exposed him to the reality of his own childhood and how he saw his family.

'He was often publicly struggling with the level of despair, the level of poverty, spiritually, emotionally and financially in people's lives. He used to feel very drained by it so he made a decision to spend two to three days a week away from the city so he could reinvigorate himself.' Karyn believes Kennedy was a good role model. At a time when others were saying that you had to give everything to the poor and live in the mayhem of poverty, Kennedy knew they all had to sustain themselves.

For a while, Kennedy, Karyn and Peter Walsh and their 18-month-old, James (the first of their three children), shared the parish house at St Mary's. One of the scenes that James, now 24, remembers is running around the hallways and dancing with Peter Kennedy. It was a regular occurrence.

Another time, Kennedy built a fence around the property. He installed a doorbell on the outside gate, then failed to connect it. It was a futile attempt at separating himself from the chaos that so often found its way to his front door. There is a wry smile on Karyn's face as she tells the tale.

Karyn says that over time Kennedy has moved away from intense hands-on work. He still has contact with people, but Sallywattle, his retreat in the Numinbah Valley, has allowed him to develop a spirituality for justice, one that sustains people working with those on the margins, as well as those who are vulnerable.

For Karyn, St Mary's has provided much of the sustenance she has needed. She likes the rhythm of it and she feels she needs the spiritual practice in her life. 'The rest of my week is pretty busy. It pulls me in all directions.'

She adds, 'You hold on to some things because of the familiarity. I think that about the Eucharist and community really. There are parts that you feel there's something in it, even though it's changed over the years, there are parts that have always been there.' The diversity at St Mary's appeals to Karyn too. But there's also what she refers to as a 'steadiness'—the Word, the breaking of the bread, communion. Being part of the parish for more than 20 years, she has watched her own children and the children of others grow up.

'And we're getting older, many of us, together.' There are many treasures she believes to be found in a faith community.

One of the aspects of St Mary's that really engaged Karyn was the congregation's decision to respond to the local environment, not in ad hoc ways, but strategically, as a parish. St Mary's is located next door to the OZ Care men's hostel, a shelter for homeless men, and it is in an area where many indigenous people meet. At times, church-goers on their way to Mass would literally have to step over inebriated people who had passed out on the pavement. The task was to decide how best to respond; what action to take.

Karyn became an integral part of the discernment process. 'We always talk about responding to injustice, but we also need to value creating, celebrating and promoting justice.' Karyn vividly remembers one woman from St Mary's who confessed her concern at not having much time to do something for refugees. Karyn was amazed. She still is as she retells the story. The woman had a disabled child, she was also looking after her elderly mother, and she had a husband with mental illness.

A not-for-profit organisation was set up at St Mary's in 1995. It became Micah Projects – usually referred to simply as Micah – and, in a bid to remain independent, it was not established under the auspices of the Catholic Archdiocese. What began as a very small local service, heavily dependent on St Mary's church for support, little more than a decade later employs now over 100 staff. It caters for homeless people; those with addictions; women who have experienced domestic violence; people who have experienced sexual abuse within the Catholic Church; young mothers; and people with mental health or disability issues. Karyn has been with the service since its inception and her title of coordinator is misleading. She is actually in charge of Micah Projects on a day-to-day basis; that is, she is responsible for staff and a myriad of hands-on projects.

Karyn sits at her desk looking at her computer through her dark-rimmed glasses. She has a small office crammed with a desk and computer, a table with four chairs, and a long cabinet stacked with books, files, manuals and manila folders. Any attempt at neatness has given way to clutter. Three separate doorways lead into her office. Through them there is a steady flow of human traffic.

Coordinating the not-for-profit organisation is a challenge, one that Karyn has happily embraced. She is proud of the number of people whose lives Micah has contributed to. Some of the people who originally came to the organisation in need of support, or out of desperation, are now part of Micah's staff.

While government funding these days enables Micah to provide many valuable services, Karyn believes, 'We have really shared in people's humanity and witnessed their amazing spirit in the face of adversity . . . the same spirit that we call upon as we live with those we love and deal with the highs and lows of everyday life.'

With the dispute between the Archbishop of Brisbane and Kennedy, there was some concern about the future of Micah. Its administrative offices have long been located in the parish house at St Mary's. While Kennedy had to leave the church building of St Mary's by late April 2009, Micah was permitted to stay in the parish house a few months longer. When I spoke to Karyn in late May, Micah had already secured new administrative premises. With its services spread out around South Brisbane, she thought the main impact of the move would be paying higher rent.

Although Micah was an initiative of St Mary's parish, Karyn says that Kennedy has not had any need to control it. But being in the church grounds means that in recent times Karyn has found herself responding to media phone calls and attending to a barrage of visitors. 'I've been very involved in the whole debacle,' she says.

In 2004, when there was some concern over baptisms performed at St Mary's, Karyn went to see Archbishop Bathersby. While she felt a couple of the Archbishop's comments about St Mary's were 'a bit exaggerated', it was by her account a cordial conversation. She felt she was listened to. She also recalls the Archbishop saying that every diocese needs a place for people who struggle in the mainstream church.

Of recent events she comments, 'I am disappointed that this whole conflict has bypassed the community. It has reduced St Mary's to the priest – when it is so much more. This really disappoints me because our faith and strength as a community has been ignored and reduced to "being a flock". The Archbishop could have engaged with the community first before using all the power he has to sack Peter Kennedy . . . Who knows what could have come from that experience. I suppose I should not be shocked because I have experienced it so often in the Catholic Church; the voice of the people is ignored in the name of doctrine and protecting the Church by men with power. So in the end it is power and status that wins, not faith.'

Karyn will continue to work through the ramifications of recent events as a respected voice at St Mary's-in-Exile. It's where she feels she belongs.

TERRY FITZPATRICK

It is the day before Fr Peter Kennedy and Fr Terry Fitzpatrick celebrate their last liturgical service at St Mary's in South Brisbane. Fitzpatrick stands on the porch of the old wooden parish house that has become home to Micah Projects, the social-justice initiative of the parish. Wearing a blue swirly T-shirt that could be a remnant of the 1960s, he slings his backpack on the floor. Fitzpatrick feels at home here. That's not surprising. He has been at St Mary's since 1994 and he has been a part of Micah since its fledgling beginnings in 1995.

As we talk, a fellow who has been on the streets for weeks wanders in. Fitzpatrick interrupts our conversation. He offers the man a cup of tea, asks his name, and has a chat. Fitzpatrick then asks the fellow to wait on the verandah while he organises assistance. On return Fitzpatrick tells him that Karyn will look after him, soon. She'll help him find a place to stay. Fitzpatrick returns to the update he is giving me on recent events between the Catholic Church and St Mary's. Briefly.

'Any chance of a new shirt?' pipes up the homeless man, whose sense of boundary or protocol has given way to his own urgent needs. 'We'll see what we can do,' responds Fitzpatrick, leading him back out to the verandah.

Most days it's hard for Fitzpatrick to get past reception at the old church house, without someone needing him for something pressing. He's often in demand at Micah. Yet he's also learnt how to stay centred while remaining open and present to the world around him. It has taken years to cultivate, this centredness, but it is integral to Fitzpatrick's way of being a priest.

Fitzpatrick grew up in Toowoomba in a house packed with nine children. It was somewhere between a shed full of machinery in which his father, a cabinet-maker, plied his trade, and the shop at the front of the house which sold the products of his father's labour. Working at home and helping in the shop were givens in the Fitzpatrick family. So was religion. The Catholic church was 400 metres up the road. Fitzpatrick's father went to Mass every morning, taking a few kids along with him. Parents and children were part of the larger church congregation on Sunday mornings, and like many his age, Fitzpatrick served as an altar boy. 'I just loved ringing those bells. It was so expressive.' A smile appears on his face.

Sport had its place too. His parents encouraged it. School, Fitzpatrick felt, was there to provide opportunities for sport. Cricket and football matches are etched in his mind. The same, however, could not be said of his studies. 'There was too much living to do to be sitting around doing assignments,' he quips before laughing at the thought of not being able to actually recall doing one single assignment. What he does remember is cramming the night before exams. Somehow it worked. He passed secondary school.

Although Fitzpatrick had thoughts of becoming a priest, instead of theological studies he chose nursing, as had his sister and his aunty. It was only once he had moved to Princess Alexandra Hospital in Brisbane that he realised that he hadn't lived in a city before. The parameters of Fitzpatrick's life were no longer defined by the family home, the sports field, the school and the church. He was glimpsing a much bigger world. And he was now on his own.

His training and residence were both in the hospital. It became the centre of his world. But being confronted by life and death on a regular basis, he began to reflect, to ask some of the bigger questions. They were the sort of questions that you have to find your own answers to.

After graduating as a nurse, Fitzpatrick became a full-time youth worker. He lived in a community where members took commitment and service seriously. Part of that commitment was converting people to Jesus. During his nursing studies he'd become involved in the charismatic movement within the Catholic Church, so this trajectory seemed a natural one. Six of the men in the community went into the seminary. Fitzpatrick was one of the six. That was in 1981.

The seminary at Banyo, in the northern suburbs of Brisbane, had a powerful effect on the new recruit. It introduced him to aspects of religion and faith he had never heard of. The way he tells it, there were three defining moments. Although his memory of which year they occurred is hazy, the experiences remain vivid.

The first. A week-long Zen Buddhist retreat for seminarians. Fitzpatrick sat on his mat, incense wafting, listening to the eastern bells being rung, and bowed as he had been taught. The sacredness of the practice enthralled him. He was immediately drawn by the contemplative aspect of Buddhism, captured by its beauty. It was unlike anything he had experienced.

But perhaps what is more surprising, in the light of recent events at St Mary's, is that the man he sat next to for eight days on that retreat was the spiritual director of the seminary, Fr John Bathersby, now the Archbishop of Brisbane.

After the retreat, Fitzpatrick set up his own Zendo place in the seminary, in a spare room downstairs – a place used for private Masses. The Zen practice had opened a door to contemplation, to being present in any given moment. He learnt how to really sit for meditation, how to empty the mind. He also discovered the concept of embracing paradox. He couldn't help reflecting on it, and continues to do so decades later. The Zen experience also taught him to respect diversity.

The second. Towards the end of first year, as exams loomed, the young seminarian was asked by his superiors to look after some guests. It was not something Fitzpatrick wanted to do. Not something of interest. He certainly had other priorities – cramming. But realising there was no-one else to look after the visitors, he decided to put his mind to it.

One of those visitors was Carl Jasper, author, teacher and lay theologian. He was visiting with some Columban priests from the Philippines. Fitzpatrick found them so vibrant, so alive, so full of stories of people whose desperate poverty had not quelled their spirit or their determination to make something out of their lives, that he was awestruck. 'They talked about challenging unjust structures. I sat with them, from five o'clock until after midnight. It was one of those moments of change. Afterwards, you just know that you are different.'

But Fitzpatrick soon learnt that structural justice was not just something for the Philippines, and other faraway places.

The third. Electrical workers in Queensland were losing their jobs to casual contract labour. The workers felt they had to stand up for their rights so they went on strike. 'There were blackouts on and off for months. We (some of the seminarians) joined the picket. This was where the Gospel called us . . . Standing on the picket line with these guys, I thought we might get arrested . . . but it was a moment of taking a stand.' Some people objected to the seminarians' stance. There were abusive telephone calls and letters to his superiors. Yet it was a transforming event for Fitzpatrick.

Soon after, while doing a pastoral stint in the prison, he met Kennedy – priest and prison chaplain. Within a year, he asked Kennedy to be his spiritual director. What drew him to Kennedy was his honesty, his upfront approach and his lack of piety. The two talked about their lives and about what kept them going. It was all very real. Perhaps too real for some.

According to Fitzpatrick, more than eight of the seminarians Kennedy was spiritual director to, left the seminary. Suspecting spiritual direction may not be his best role, Kennedy approached the spiritual director of the seminary, Bathersby. Bathersby recognised Kennedy as a different voice, respected him, and still wanted him around. Later, when Bathersby was offered the position of bishop, Kennedy was one of the people he consulted. What were his thoughts? At that time, Kennedy thought Bathersby would make a good bishop.

After years in the seminary, Fitzpatrick enjoyed his new role which included being out in country Queensland parishes. It was refreshing. And the people liked him. But things didn't quite go to plan.

Fitzpatrick was a Catholic priest who, unlike most, fathered a child. But having done so, Fitzpatrick dismissed church lawyers' advice to have no contact with his son. He wanted to care for him, to actively parent. Leaving the priesthood was certainly on his mind. It was a time of intense discernment. He sought solitude at Kennedy's bush retreat, Sallywattle, in the Numinbah Valley, an hour or so from Brisbane. On occasion he also talked to Kennedy. Kennedy's advice, that Fitzpatrick could still be a priest if he really wanted to, resonated.

Fitzpatrick returned to study in Brisbane, this time to do a masters in social work. While there, after two unsuccessful attempts by a bishop to place Fitzpatrick in a suitable parish, he began working at St Mary's. That was 1994. He's been there ever since.

The congregation willingly took on a Catholic priest with a son, but it was the parish priest, Peter Kennedy, more than anyone else who had to do quite a bit of adjusting. Fitzpatrick describes Kennedy as a man who seeks solitude. 'He's an enormously private person, but when he's with people, he's right out there. Afterwards, though, he has to withdraw.'

Kennedy and Fitzpatrick shared a house. At first having two-year-old Jordan around the house several days a week was difficult for Kennedy. He wasn't used to it. But a year on, Kennedy began to take a more active role, entering into a relationship with the child. It was a relationship which grew. Kennedy soon found himself in circumstances he had never imagined. Here is one example.

It was some time after the weapons amnesty following the Port Arthur massacre. Jordan, like many children, had been encouraged to hand in his toy weapons. Kennedy and the young child are out shopping. The child asks for something. 'No, you can't have a kill toy,' says Kennedy with an air of authority. The child persists. So does Kennedy. Finally, a passer-by intervenes. 'Get with it grandpa. He's asking for a cool toy, not a kill toy.'

The relationship between Kennedy and Fitzpatrick grew too. They saw the world in similar ways. For them contemplation and social justice were central to following Jesus. They became a great support to each other and understood each other well. They cared about each other and also discussed many things. But they didn't want to just say the right words. They wanted to support their community to be people of action.

Six months after moving to St Mary's, Fitzpatrick was appointed by Archbishop Bathersby to the Murri Ministry, a team of Aboriginal and non-Aboriginal people. It is a position he has relished. Shortly after, the social-justice initiative of St Mary's, Micah Projects was established. Fitzpatrick has been involved since its inception. He's seen it flourish, and empower many people.

The principle of empowerment spread inside the church at St Mary's too. It became a place that welcomed all, and encouraged participation regardless of gender, sexual orientation, class, culture, marital status, race or religion. In the secular world this may be applauded. But, according to church authorities, it is not the Catholic way.

Fitzpatrick, like most of the congregation at St Mary's, has supported Kennedy all through the conflict with Archbishop Bathersby.

There has been a history of conflict between bishops or archbishops and the religious personnel at St Mary's. In 1879, Mary MacKillop, whose sisters had taken over the school at St Mary's nine years prior, was forced to withdraw her sisters from Brisbane because of a dispute with the bishop. An official report which hung inside St Mary's church reads: '16 December, 1879. The sisters leave their convent in South Brisbane attended by a large number of men, women and children, and go to the wharf of the ASN company for their departure from Brisbane.'

Although the times, the context and the characters involved in the recent conflict are different, almost one hundred and thirty years later, in April 2009, there was another procession that left St Mary's. This time, however, it was the congregation and its two priests. Their destination was the Trades and Labour Council (TLC) building, a temporary locale until a more suitable abode could be found. Fitzpatrick, who along with Kennedy led the community, says, 'We walked as people of faith, into uncertainty. But we did it together.'

JOHN AND GWENNETH ROBERTS

It's Sunday morning at St Mary's. Two large bunches of brightly coloured balloons filled with helium are tethered to the altar. The microphones are checked, the choir is practising, and there's an air of expectation, perhaps excitement. This will be the last Sunday morning service for Fr Peter Kennedy, Fr Terry Fitzpatrick and their congregation inside the church at St Mary's.

Half a dozen people are on the altar making last-minute preparations. Among them are John and Gwenneth Roberts. Forty-seven years of marriage and six children have not dented their zest for life, but enhanced it. Wearing a yellow shirt with 'St Mary's Matters' emblazoned in black lettering across the back, the diminutive Gwenneth, an extrovert by nature, is easily spotted. So too her husband, John, the taller, more introverted of the couple. He is also wearing a St Mary's shirt which is green.

When the service begins, Gwenneth stands with the choir, while John sits on the long wooden seat behind the pulpit facing the congregation. In his hand is a stick with a sign glued to it. It reads, 'The Spirit gives LIFE. The Law KILLS.' The sign is Gwenneth's handiwork. It is homemade and handwritten. And it attracts attention, not just because of the wording, but because it is the only placard in the entire congregation.

One might not expect the only people carrying a placard in the church to be a physician and a doctor of philosophy. But what is perhaps more surprising is that they are Anglican. Anglicans who, after a journey spanning decades, dioceses and religious diversity, found their way to St Mary's, to be a part of what they feel is a dynamic community. But had it not been for John's father, Harry Roberts, that journey might never have eventuated.

In 1946, when the founder of The Church of England Grammar School – now known as The Anglican Church Grammar School or Churchie – in East Brisbane, was retiring, he asked Harry Roberts, then headmaster of Toowoomba Grammar School, to take over the position. Although Harry Roberts came from a Methodist background he had been baptised Presbyterian for reasons his son is still unsure of. A condition of employment, however, was Anglican faith. Harry accepted. Archbishop Halse then confirmed Harry privately. 'My father believed he was Christian first, and denomination was of secondary importance,' says John. It is a legacy John too has embraced.

John and Gwenneth met at the Princess Alexandra hospital where they worked. John was a doctor, Gwenneth a registered nurse. They married in 1962. Although both were raised Anglican, Gwenneth's experience of church life and confirmation felt meaningless. It wasn't until they began having children that they looked for a church to attend.

When they later moved to Melbourne, John and Gwenneth joined a lively evangelical Anglican parish in Ivanhoe, not far from the Repatriation Hospital where John was based. It was a time of intense scriptural learning and involvement. Some of the congregation participated in the Billy Graham Crusades. But it was the vicar's wife who really influenced Gwenneth. 'She was so caring, always praying for so many people.' Gwenneth, who describes her experience as a gradual spiritual awakening, says it was at this time that she felt she needed to make a commitment to Christ.

If the trip back to Brisbane was any indication of what lay ahead for the couple, then they were in for a rough ride. It was 1969. Three small children and a three-month-old baby along with two adults and supplies for the three-day journey were packed into the little Cortina. 'We hadn't even made it past Pentridge, on Bell Street (7 kilometres), when the Cortina blew a gasket,' says John, laughing at the scene that is etched in his memory. Still, they continued, filling the radiator every few kilometres. 'It was near Seymour that the car just had it. I found a service station and Gwen ran over to the motel. Luckily the fellow fixed the car the next day.'

On return to Brisbane, they settled in Mt Gravatt, where they stayed for most of the 1970s. It was a newly emerging suburb and had an Anglican evangelical church that suited. The Roberts family founded the church's 36-piece orchestra, with all six of their children playing instruments. John took up double bass. Gwenneth accompanied them on piano.

But it was a young priest, a fellow with a passion for social justice, who made them really think. That priest's name was Ray Barraclough. And he didn't like all that Queensland premier Jo Bjelke-Petersen stood for. John recalls Barraclough saying, 'If I don't turn up tomorrow, I'll probably have been arrested for protesting, so take the service for me.' Gwenneth says, 'We were scriptural people and Ray and his wife expanded the scriptures for us in a way we'd never heard of. They incorporated social justice into our belief system.' They also introduced the Roberts to an Aboriginal woman, Aunty Jean Phillips. It is a relationship which has grown over the years, as has their understanding and support for Aboriginal people and the issues that confront them.

By the early 1980s, the family had moved to a large Federation house in Greenslopes with sweeping views of the city from the front verandah. But Gwenneth felt an intellectual restlessness. It was time for her to move out of her more traditional role.

Returning to study after an absence of 25 years was not easy. While studying her Bachelor of Business in health administration, Gwenneth met Dr Patricia Brennan who had established the Movement for the Ordination of Women in the Anglican Church. Gwenneth thought Brennan made so much sense that she convened the Queensland branch of the movement. 'From then on I was radicalised,' says Gwenneth. 'I saw the oppression of women in the Anglican Church.'

Gwenneth was one of many who stood outside Anglican cathedrals with banners and sang songs of protest. John often accompanied her. She describes it as a long bitter struggle, one that was ecumenical, with the Catholic Mercy sisters supporting the Anglican women. It was also a time in which John and Gwenneth learnt a lot about church politics; how heated and how bitter it can become. And they learnt about church history. 'I realised that women were not excluded from church leadership in the early church,' says John.

After Gwenneth graduated, at 50 years of age, she began working for Queensland Health, working on breast and cervical cancer statistics. Three months into the project she was diagnosed with breast cancer. Dealing with statistics is one thing, but living with the disease is another. John says, 'There was no point saying to Gwenneth, well your doctor says you have a 95 per cent chance of surviving five years, because she'd say, "But you don't know if I'm in the five per cent that does." What she needed was care and support.'

She recalls a friend whose father had had cancer giving her advice. 'Just stay there until God tells you otherwise. And don't count yourself as a statistic, just have faith.' Those words are as meaningful to her today as they were back in 1988. As he always has, John stood by his wife, cared for her and supported her. Gwenneth had a mastectomy and was back at work within a month.

Soon after, she became involved in a government taskforce on domestic violence, and it was in this field that she went on to research and earn her PhD. Since then she has been a ground-breaking researcher and educator for the medical profession on the issue.

When John and Gwenneth first moved to Greenslopes, they had joined an Anglican church close to town. Realising the minister was not interested in Gwenneth's attempts at education on Aboriginal issues, and recognising that the struggle for women's ordination in the Anglican church had taken a toll on Gwenneth, the couple decided it was time to look elsewhere for a church that accepted their beliefs.

Having heard about St Mary's through their son, Tim, who was involved in music production at the church, they decided to go along. It was different from what they were used to. John was hesitant, but Gwenneth knew she'd found what she was searching for. 'I was accepted for who I was . . . It's the best experience of ecumenism I've had. You're accepted if you're black or white, gay, lesbian, Baptist or whatever.' John and Gwenneth also liked the informality and the role of women in the life and practices of that church. John says, 'They weren't interested if you were Catholic or Calathumpian, but if you were interested in this ministry, in being part of the community, you were welcome.' For Gwenneth it was a healing time.

John and Gwenneth don't always agree with the theology at St Mary's, but for them that is not the point. They see St Mary's as a place for questioning and discussing, and for diversity. They also see it as a place where the priests share the pulpit with the lay people and draw on the vast experience in the congregation.

John was deeply moved listening to a homily given by Robert Perrier, a parishioner who spoke of his experience through depression, and of what it meant for him to now count himself as part of St Mary's.

On the occasion of their 40th wedding anniversary, John and Gwenneth were invited to give a homily. They didn't attempt to tell anyone else how to live. It was a reflection: on their approach, their way, and what had worked for them. It was also an opportunity to give thanks, to each other and to their community.

St Mary's has become an important part of John and Gwenneth's lives. When their own children left home, they mentioned to Kennedy that they would like to offer their home as a place of hospitality, as part of their Christian commitment; not just for fundraising evenings, recitals, and other parish events. This is something they still do. But they also wanted to offer long-term hospitality.

Their first guest was a young student lawyer from Malaysia whose scholarship was cut during the last economic crisis. St Mary's paid some of his fees, and the Roberts offered him a home. He stayed a year. John still talks about the delicious curries he used to cook. Other guests have included an Aboriginal family, and a young couple with a baby. Once again Gwenneth and John welcomed them. Like other guests, the couple and their child have become part of the Roberts' extended family.

Gwenneth also remembers when her brother had come to live with them. He was dying. She put a folding bed out on the verandah for her brother to lie on during the day, in the winter sun. By his side was a chair where Gwenneth sat, reading him *The Tao of Pooh*. He loved it. Fr Terry Fitzpatrick also sat with him. 'I used to leave them alone so Terry could minister to him. Terry was so lovely, so caring, and very present to him. He even dressed up formally for my brother's funeral,' says Gwenneth, an emotional tone resonating in her voice.

After the last Sunday-morning service for the congregation inside the church building at St Mary's, John and Gwenneth took part in the two-block procession down to the TLC building – their new, temporary place of worship. Gwenneth walked with the choir. John, placard aloft, walked among the crowd that stretched four or five abreast.

Like many other parishioners, they are sad to leave the old church, but John and Gwenneth, the two priests, Kennedy and Fitzpatrick, and hundreds of others will continue their liturgies at the TLC building. Gwenneth speaks with conviction: 'It's the people who are the church. We chose to leave our tradition, but most of the people at St Mary's didn't. They were forced out. But we'll continue to support each other and minister to each other. It's a faith-filled community.'

GEMMA GREEN

Gemma Green relaxes on the porch of her Brisbane home. She is wearing a pink top, which like her personality is bright and at times shines. Draped over her top is a light-weight jacket. One of the buttons on her jacket is buttoned and unbuttoned many times during our two-hour conversation. It appears to be a reflex action, one which occurs when she is deep in thought, contemplating how best to respond. Green may well be a thinker, one who likes intellectual stimulation, but the rigours of family life leave little time for that.

As a mother of five, time to herself is a luxury. This particular Sunday afternoon when we meet, three of her teenage children are downstairs milling about. She sits on the settee and begins telling stories. They are often accompanied by her broad smile. And in that smile one detects traces of a spirited country girl.

Green grew up in Warwick, not far from the Queensland–New South Wales border. One of seven children, Green's family upbringing was strict Irish Catholic. Her mother was devout, so devout that her father, originally Church of England, converted to marry her mother.

Ever since Green can remember, her mother went to Mass every morning. It was a practice the daughter, like the rest of the family, respected. Green lived in Warwick until she went to university. That was in 1976. While she was discovering university life in Brisbane, she continued attending Mass. She liked the repetition of ritual. 'It was something that doesn't change.' And the idea of connecting with other people who believe the same thing appealed.

It is not unusual for people to define their lives or careers in stages. For Green there was the 'pre-baby' stage in which she was a biochemist. Then came the 'between babies' era in which she became a speech and drama teacher. And 'post-babies' she started her own business, Passion for Italy, selling Italian destinations. One of the benefits of the business is that she goes to Italy once or twice a year.

Most of the year, however, Green resides in Brisbane. And church has remained an important part of her life. She was an active parishioner, starting many committees in her local Catholic parish. She always wanted to feel part of a community. 'I was always searching for more, for depth, for meaning. I knew I needed spiritual support.' But eventually there came a time when she realised that it just wasn't working.

It may not be coincidental that the time she discovered her church community was not as nourishing as she needed it to be, was at the same time as her 20-year marriage ended. Green had five children at home at the time of her separation, the youngest five and six years of age, and the challenges of being a single parent soon became apparent. Green describes it as a time of great soul-searching. Many of the values and parts of her life she'd thought of as 'givens' were now being questioned. And wearing the mantel of 'divorced' at the local church did little to alleviate her discontent.

It was at this time that a friend invited her to go along to St Mary's church in South Brisbane. 'I remember being blown away the first time I went there,' she says, her face lighting up at the memory of it.

'I felt like I'd come home; found my tribe. There was acceptance for who you are, not who you have to be . . . And it didn't matter that I was divorced.' Green's enthusiasm for St Mary's was shared by her children. 'They loved it. The sermons were interesting, the music was good, and the more casual atmosphere suited . . . There was always a bit of extra entertainment too, with a few drunks coming in.'

She tells one story that is special to her. It begins back in her old parish. A fellow with mental-health issues, looking dishevelled, enters the church and lies down at the front of the altar. No-one makes a move. No-one says or does anything. Mass continues. Although people have to step over him to go to communion, the man is totally ignored. Green shudders at the thought of it. 'It was so embarrassing.'

The next part of the story takes place at St Mary's. Green had only been there a few times. Fr Fitzpatrick is giving a sermon. A homeless schizophrenic man walks in, makes his way directly to the chalice and gulps down the wine. Everyone stops. The sense of disbelief is palpable. Without a second thought, Fr Peter Kennedy gets up from a pew, walks over, takes the man by the hand and leads him back to sit beside him. With each of the homeless man's subsequent outbursts, Kennedy not only holds his hand, but pats it. Calms him down.

'That really did it for me.' This tiny act of kindness won Kennedy and St Mary's a special place in Green's heart. She believed this was what Catholicism should be – inclusive, accepting, and able to embrace all.

Over the next five years Green was content with St Mary's. She'd found the community she'd long been in search of. She established a close friendship with a group of five women who met regularly after Sunday evening Mass. 'It felt like we were family. We respected and listened to each other, and due to study and reading books like *The Power of Now*, we were trying to grow spiritually.'

Once when St Mary's was under fire for what Green describes as the priest using incorrect words during a baptism, she wrote to the Archbishop of Brisbane, contending that language changes over time, but the meaning remains. It was her church, her community, one she believed in and was happy to defend. But in 2008 something changed.

She recalls that due to pressure from the Archbishop, Fitzpatrick had begun to wear the alb when celebrating Mass. She thought that was fine. Not too much to ask. But when she returned after a one-month trip to find he had dispensed with wearing vestments, apart from the stole, she saw this as an ominous sign of what was to come.

When the situation between Kennedy and the Archbishop intensified, Green was one of the 500-strong congregation who attended a public meeting. She was the last speaker. Her speech was passionate. She implored the congregation to stay in the Catholic Church. 'They won't compromise. We'll have to be the ones to compromise.' Green thought she would be seen as a conservative voice, but her wish was to stay in the tradition and culture that was bestowed on her at birth. She soon became disappointed and angry because of all the conflict. 'At times I wondered if Peter Kennedy knew he would be thrown out if he didn't compromise.'

'I can agree with both sides,' she explains. But in this conflict there was no middle ground for people at St Mary's. The way Green saw it, her choice was to stay with the Catholic Church, or to follow the rest of the community of St Mary's down to the T.L.C building. But she didn't want to become a Protestant, so she opted to stay with the Catholic Church.

It is a very real dilemma for Green. Two of her children go to Catholic secondary schools and she wants to bring up her children in the Catholic Church. It's also a dilemma for young families who would like their children's baptisms and other sacraments recognised by the Catholic Church.

Green now feels isolated because she has lost the community that she loved. It won't be easy for her to go back to suburban parish life. She knows that. 'I'm on my own again. I'd like to find a parish with a priest with Peter Kennedy's philosophy, but they are few and far between.'

What's more, all of the group of friends from St Mary's she meets on Sunday nights have become a part of St Mary's-in-Exile. She continues to catch up with them, but it's not the same. Speaking about the broader St Mary's congregation, Green says, 'I'm not the only one who didn't go with Kennedy, but I don't know of anyone else my age who didn't.'

For Green it's important to stay inside the Catholic Church. To have a voice inside the church. There are issues she believes in, that she wants to fight for, like the ordination of women, and married clergy. A practical woman, she considers this is a long-term goal. 'Perhaps it will be for my daughter's daughter.'

One senses that Green will be pondering her own spiritual future over the coming months. But she is not alone. Near the end of the interview we head downstairs to the kitchen for a cup of tea. Green's youngest daughter is there. The previous week, she wrote a piece on St Mary's for school. It was an evaluation of one of the many articles about St Mary's that ran in the Queensland newspaper *The Courier-Mail*. Green is hoping to get her younger children involved in the local church youth group. They've been there already.

Ever courteous, Green offers me a lift to the airport. I accept. As we head towards the driveway her daughter pipes up, 'Mum, when you come back, can you take me to St Mary's?'

ROBERT PERRIER

It's 10 a.m. on a bright Brisbane wintery morning. Sun is steaming into the upstairs room where Robert Perrier is sitting. It seems to have cajoled his creativity. He's just worked out the melody of a brand new song and written the first verse in blue pen on a lined piece of paper. All that eludes him is the final phrase.

Five minutes into the interview I am treated to an impromptu performance. He leans forward and strums the guitar. His reddish hair with little ringlets drapes his forehead as he peers through his dark-rimmed glasses reading lyrics yet to be committed to memory. He has a theatrical voice, one that comes from appreciable depth. The words, like the sentiments in his song, are emotive, honest and not without humour.

> I saw the cumulus building dark in the west,
> You sensed the cleansing rain and felt we were blessed.
> I put on my macintosh, you got undressed.
> You by the fire, me . . .

A slight pause. The last chord lingers. '*Depressed.*' The final word slides into place.

Perrier is a man who has lived life fully and reflected on it. He may have left school at 14 years of age, but that did not tarnish his appetite to learn, to explore, to create, or to perform. He has had decades of experience in theatre: acting, innovating and mentoring. He's at home whether performing Shakespeare or mentoring energy-charged child gymnasts in the Flying Fruit Fly Circus. For him, theatre is about community enhancement and development.

He's also a gifted writer, one who draws on his own experiences and insights. Here is one example. It is from the opening page of a manuscript he has begun writing about his own life.

'When I first saw Scotty's aerial gyration, I understood there were at least two types of acrobat. One was compact and sprung like a golf ball. The other was lithe and loose. The former held on to power. The latter maintained only as much tension as was required to lift off and let go. The first was about quantity and danger, the latter about elegance and freedom; one could be explained, the other defied description; one was material, the other was spiritual.'

The spiritual has been an integral part of Perrier's life since his early fifties. He is part of St Mary's in South Brisbane, regularly attending Mass, and the Buddhist meditation group which was held in the church on Monday evenings. For Fr Peter Kennedy's last Sunday service inside St Mary's church, Perrier sang a song he wrote especially for the event. He was honoured to do so. There are a lot of things about St Mary's he loves: the liturgies, the work they do, the invitation to explore spirituality, and that everyone is welcome. As such, he'll stay with the community whether housed in a church or in an office building. It's not the building or the walls, but what takes place within them that matters most to him.

Perrier's journey from his childhood days being marched to Mass, to his arrival at St Mary's has been lengthy, intricate and highly emotional. Perrier paints a picture of the family he grew up in. There was frequent punishment, usually in response to arbitrary dictates. What was acceptable one day was a punishable offence the next. 'And often the punishment was life-threatening.' His father, a violent alcoholic, unleashed his anger with such severity and regularity that Perrier's mother and her three sons were always on guard. They were easily accessible targets. 'I didn't know what to feel or think.' Like other children of alcoholics and addicts, he learnt to survive on his wits, to block emotions, to detach.

His father's addictions, alcohol and gambling, consumed his weekly income. This was in a time when fathers were generally the breadwinners, and women tended the home and the children. Yet Perrier's mother worked for 20 years on the 'pineapple line' in the local Brisbane cannery. Her wage ensured that her children had food and clothing.

To the outside world it may have seemed that theirs was a regular family. But for the children, the secret of their father's addictions was another burden they carried as they were marched off to Mass each Sunday morning, dressed in collar and tie. Although his father no longer attended Mass he ensured his children did. The hypocrisy of being sent to Catholic church each week by the man who beat them is not lost on Perrier.

Perrier left school at 14. He just couldn't wait to get away from home. He also wanted to get out into the world. By the time he went to the Victorian College of the Arts in Melbourne at 26 years of age, he had already worked for Murdoch Press as a message boy, a proofreader's assistant, and proofreader. He'd been involved in the trade union movement, and he'd performed with some of Queensland's up-and-coming poets, politicians and actors.

'I wanted a get-out-of-adolescence card so I sought out adults,' Perrier says. A friend once commented that Perrier wanted wisdom without having to go through too much. But perhaps Perrier had already been through more than enough for his age.

After completing his studies at the Victorian College of the Arts, he established the Murray River Performing Group, now called Hothouse Theatre, and the Flying Fruit Fly Circus. The latter was an initiative designed to take 10 children from 10 schools around Albury Wodonga, on the Victoria–New South Wales border, and train them in circus performance under the guidance of professional circus performers. Within a short while an invitation arrived to perform at the Vancouver International Children's Festival. It was an exciting time. 'Most of the kids had never been out of Albury–Wodonga.' They were the hit of the festival. On return to Australia, the longevity of the Flying Fruit Fly Circus was ensured when it was established, not as the offshoot of another theatre company, but in its own right.

Perrier is a man for whom accolades and awards are not out of the ordinary, but he believes these accomplishments have not been the most formative aspect of his life. At times, he is reticent to talk about them. The way he sees it, he constructed a persona who could do anything. He didn't see problems. He saw opportunities.

Yet despite his success, he always felt emotionally insecure and vulnerable. 'I was in utter denial. I ran away from the traumatic events of my childhood and convinced myself that I was above and beyond it. Everything was fine for me while everything went well and went my way.' This may have been beneficial for the projects he worked on, but it was to Perrier's detriment. The more successful he became, the more successful he felt he had to be. As he looks back, he realises it was a façade, the illusion being that he saw each success as a triumph over his childhood trauma.

In the decades that followed, Perrier was a freelancer, working on festivals and events in Australia and overseas. He also ventured into management. But his past lurked like a shadow. Emotions he believed well buried, eventually surfaced. When they did he wasn't sure how to deal with them. He became severely depressed. And it got worse. Eventually he was no longer able to work.

'Today, I truly believe I had to have a major breakdown to jolt me out of the denial. It was a choice of life or death. I seriously thought about taking my life. The breakdown manifested itself in various ways but effectively it was a decade of progressive depression, which is really the refusal to feel, just as denial is the refusal to know.'

After building a successful career, the breakdown was not where he had imagined life would take him. It led him to complete social isolation. For eight months he slept on cardboard cartons and newspapers. By day he walked the streets of Brisbane convincing himself that a world without people wasn't that bad. He knew where he could get hot showers and food and where he could get books. But one day he found himself with a group of people with similar histories and similar problems and for the first time in his life he didn't feel he needed the answers to everything. It was as if he had found a form of freedom he never knew existed.

It was liberating. A time of transformation. He sought help. This included long-term intensive therapy. Through therapy he was able to revisit the emotional trauma of his childhood and adolescence, and to see it in a more mature, more life-sustaining way.

'I'm not as afraid or as anxious. I don't feel the need to control my emotional state or environment. I'm much more able to suffer feelings, mine and others, which makes for a more engaging and fulfilling life.' He now lives with an openness that eluded him for decades.

Part of his transformation has been the realisation of his need for spiritual nourishment. He believes that the emotional and the spiritual are intrinsically linked. Having been brought up Catholic, the first stop on his spiritual search was the cathedral. There was a familiarity about it. He didn't go for the ritual. He went to listen to the choir. It was so soothing. Then one day, as he was passing St Mary's he saw the social-justice signs outside so he went in.

He liked St Mary's from his first visit. 'I thought it was a good place to come. The sense of community was strong . . . I'm a lapsed Catholic who goes to church. I feel a connection with the community and their work. There is something very special about the way they do Eucharist. They don't intellectualise it.'

St Mary's is a natural fit for Perrier. There's a certain 'madness', a kind of freedom that he likes. He's not a fan of the Roman Catholic Church as an institution. He sees its control as too stifling. Too rigid. He's a creative person, open to experience. That's how he likes his faith community to be too.

Of St Mary's he says: 'One doesn't get the impression that it's run by anyone, and certainly not by an institution. There doesn't seem to be a great deal of organisation but everything that needs to get done, gets done.' He also likes the diversity, from the conservative to the eccentric. He counts himself among the latter. But regardless of where people are on that continuum, St Mary's makes space for them. It welcomes them and invites them to share their stories.

One day Perrier gave a homily at St Mary's, and told the story of his life on the streets. He'd found a garage that he could sleep in. It belonged to a chemist. He'd wait until the chemist left of an evening then roll out newspapers and cartons and his sleeping bag on the asphalt floor. That was his bed. Once when it was raining, he left the cardboard and newspapers inside the garage. Since they were still there when he returned next evening he continued this practice. Sometime before Christmas, when he'd found the help he needed, he packed up the cartons and newspapers and left them in the garage. Just after Christmas he returned to collect something he'd left nearby. When he peered into the garage for one last look, on top of the cardboard he found a plum pudding with a Christmas card. It said *Happy Christmas*, and it was handwritten.

Just before ending the homily Robert Perrier told the congregation that he came to St Mary's because here he had found a community which understood that 'love can sometimes be as simple as an anonymous plum pudding, without intent'.

It is a lesson that has not been lost on Perrier. In the week the congregation made the move from the old church to the TLC building, a drunk came in during evening Mass. He started yelling and swearing. Kennedy called people from Micah to help. He then asked Perrier if he would sit outside the church with the disturbed man until the helpers came. Perrier didn't have any hesitation. Although the man verbally threatened him at one stage—'If I wanted to, I could do you'—he wasn't afraid. Perrier stayed with him and after a while the man's demeanour calmed. The two men began to chat. Perrier reflects. 'I was able to suffer his aggression and fear and because I could we both benefited.'

Perrier has come a long way. In St Mary's he's found a place of refuge. A place where he belongs. In a song he's written for his next play, there's a line, '*Is this the end? Or just where we begin?*' One suspects that for Perrier, as with St Mary's, it's just the beginning.

MILLIE DE CONCEICAO

Millie De Conceicao treads gently on the ground as she moves about her garden, surveying the plants and vegetables. She has a keen eye, noting the tiniest change. 'I just love growing food. I always have,' she says.

She was the community garden coordinator at St Mary's. There, Millie turned the disused land around the old parish house into a flourishing organic garden. The conditions may not have been ideal – a small piece of land, part of it shaded, the soil in need of replenishment – but this gardener is not one to allow difficulties to stop her. Her own life is proof of that.

Born in East Timor, Millie was four when, in the mid-1970s, Indonesian forces invaded. 'I remember the preparations and the family packing up. I was very excited. I thought we were going on holidays.' But this was no holiday. Before long, Millie found herself squashed in the back of a truck, gunfire all around, people screaming. Separated from her family, she was taken by the Portuguese owners of the land her parents cultivated.

She remembers Fretilin soldiers on the back of the truck, trying to protect the children, telling them to keep their heads down. But Millie had a mind of her own. 'I put my head up at the wrong time. Looking out between the soldier's legs, I saw a mother holding her child, and a shot went straight through them.' Millie's immediate response was to vomit.

'From that time on, I felt my mind went into slow motion.' Neither the Portuguese family nor the Red Cross boat ride to Darwin could ease her burden. Yet in Darwin, where Millie was given permanent residency on arrival, there was a treat in store. 'The food tasted so good. I had a little tin, like a Milo tin, and I used to put some of my food in it. I was saving it for my brothers and sisters, so they could eat what I'd eaten.'

But the treasured tin she stored in a cupboard was soon discovered. '"It's for my sister," I said when they tried to take it off me. That's when I was told that I wasn't going home. I just started screaming in Tetum that I wanted to go home. I felt so scared and alone.'

From that day on, Millie's life was focused on survival.

Life with the Portuguese family was horrific. When the authorities became aware of their abusive treatment, Millie became a ward of the state. But neither the orphanage nor the string of foster-care families offered the emotional support she needed. By the time she was 15, Millie was living independently in the YWCA.

By then, Millie, an introvert with a gentle presence, had become 'an aggressive, violent young woman'. Inner conflict and lack of belonging were taking a heavy toll.

Millie had long believed that her family was dead. Killed in the conflict. That's what she'd been told. There were so many things she didn't know about herself, and had no way of finding out. She didn't even know her age. Her birth date had been changed three times by government officials. And memories of East Timor were now tucked away.

At this stage, Millie could have ended up like some of her friends: drug and suicide statistics. But she has a strong will, not only to survive, but to become a healthy, balanced human being. It was this inner drive that forced her to leave Darwin.

In Brisbane she went from job to job, but primarily she was searching for her identity and a sense of belonging. Millie even sought marriage as a way to resolve her isolation, but it didn't. The greatest solace since her late twenties were her dogs, Shadow and Lucy. 'Shadow had had a hard life. She bit me when I first got her. But I didn't hit her. I just said, "It's OK, I understand." And Lucy, she taught me so much. No matter how I felt, she was there, loving me, kissing me, and cuddling up to me.'

It was while she was living in Brisbane that Millie first met Fr Terry Fitzpatrick from St Mary's. They had met through a common friend and over time their friendship grew. Seeing a community garden Millie had created inspired Fitzpatrick. He asked if she would design and plant a vegetable garden around the old parish house at St Mary's. Millie accepted.

It wasn't just the variety of organic vegetables that she relished, but the cast of characters who dropped in. Many never ventured inside the church yet out in the vegetable patch they discovered a special space. It became a place where the homeless, those battling drug and alcohol addictions, as well as the regular weekend church-goers, mingled. 'It was a place to mix with people you might not usually meet. It felt very safe, although sometimes it was a bit of an eye-opener,' says Millie.

Working so close to the church building, she heard a lot about St Mary's and over time her suspicions that it might be worth a visit were aroused. Millie had been born into a Catholic family, but growing up in an orphanage, being forced to attend church services, had not encouraged her faith. Not in a formal way at least.

Just as Millie accepted Fitzpatrick's offer to design and set up the community garden, she accepted the invitation, somewhat reluctantly, to go inside the church. To her surprise it was a 'beautiful' experience. She also found Fr Peter Kennedy's homilies touching. 'They felt so real.' She could relate to them. 'It's what church should be. They help people feel at home, and connected.'

Recently divorced, and feeling a little lost, Millie found St Mary's to be a precious place. And while she liked the priests' homilies, she was more impressed by what they did. Millie indicates she is not the most regular attender of Sunday services – she often cares for people with spinal injuries and disabilities on the weekend – yet that does not diminish the sense of belonging she feels at St Mary's.

It was while she was working in the garden at St Mary's that Millie received news that her family in East Timor might be alive. Initially she was shocked. Should she go to East Timor? She wasn't sure. It was with this on her mind that she had a chat to Fitzpatrick.

'Terry was so keen for me to find my family. He kept encouraging me to go to East Timor, to get in touch with my roots. Terry spoke to Peter . . . They make things happen . . . Terry started collecting money for me to go to East Timor, and before I knew it, I was on the plane.' Not only did they help with the ticket but also with contacts in East Timor. Millie flew into Dili on 12 May 2004.

Within 48 hours of arrival, the one-time orphan had located her mother. 'When I saw you coming, I thought you looked just like your dad,' were her mother's words. Millie's father, who had been ill for much of his adult life, and who Millie remembers with so much affection, had died. But she visited his grave. Her two weeks in East Timor were full of reunions with brothers and sisters, nieces and nephews, extended family, and with the land the family grow their food on.

For the first time in 29 years, Millie looked just like those who surrounded her, although they no longer had a common language. 'I don't feel like them, but I do look like them – the way I sit and hold my head on the side when I'm thinking. We even have the same forehead . . . They even knew how old I am.'

Although happy to find her family, it was an emotional time, and she was surprised at her anger. It was directed at her mother, and it intensified when she began to question why she had been allowed to go with the Portuguese family, to be separated from her mother.

When she returned to Australia she began making sense of her own story. East Timor was such a powerful experience. 'In some ways, it was all a bit much,' she says reflectively. She was left with so much to ponder.

Drawn to movement and solitude, Millie rose most mornings around five o'clock to practise two hours of ballet. The movement, the stretching, and the sense of balance grounded her. On Monday evenings she often found her way to St Mary's for the Buddhist meditation group. It was a surrendering to deep inner solitude, to the sacred; a reminder to live in the present moment.

Millie grew up not having many people she could trust. But these days she has a deep sense of self, of who she is, and where she belongs. She has also found her community. Of St Mary's she says, 'I belong there. I'm accepted regardless of going along each week.'

She has been deeply saddened by what has happened to St Mary's. 'It's taking a lot of people's home away,' Millie says, conscious of the number of homeless people who have come to rely on the community garden and the church grounds. 'The church without Peter and Terry is nothing . . . We are all as one there.' Millie has been wondering how best to support the community that embraced her and has given her so much. And she's just begun thinking about her next trip to East Timor.

A shorter version of this article appeared in **The Courier-Mail.**

SAM WATSON

Sam Watson, a senior Aboriginal man who was born and raised in Brisbane, introduces himself in the traditional indigenous way.

His maternal grandparents were from the Mullenjarlie tribal nation and the Yugenby language group. Their traditional lands are to the south-west of Brisbane. He also has blood ties with the Jagara people, who are the traditional custodians of the land to the south of the Brisbane River, and the Nunuccal people from Minjerribah (Stradbroke Island). His paternal grandmother was of the Kangalu people of central Queensland and his grandfather was of the Biri Gubba people who are part of the Wirri language group. He also has blood ties to the Kalkadoon people of Mount Isa, and the Wik people of Cape York. His family extends throughout Queensland from Brisbane to Palm Island and Cherbourg, from dry inland areas to tropical coastal regions.

Watson, who was born in 1952, recalls his childhood. 'We were very poor, we rarely had electricity, and we used to sit around the candle or the hurricane lamp at night and tell stories.' He was enthralled by the yarns, the way they were told, and the humour that often accompanied them.

At a young age he discovered a passion for reading. He explains how many of his elders worked on the stock routes and used to carry books with them. When they returned to town they'd leave the books. 'Every time I went to visit an aunt or an uncle there would always be a new batch of great books to read.'

He was also told by his elders that he must work hard at school so he could one day go to university. As he reached his teenage years, however, his joy of reading was tempered by the realisation that none of the stories in the books were about Aboriginal people. It didn't seem to make sense. Why weren't the enthralling stories he had listened to by the flickering hurricane light in print?

How delighted he was when he saw his Aunty Kath's poetry in print. Printed in 1964, *We Are Going* was the first book of poems published in Australia by an indigenous poet. Aunty Kath was Kath Walker, or Oodgeroo as she became known after 1987. Aunty Kath Walker was one of the true heroes in Watson's extended family and he often visited her.

Oodgeroo was passionate, creative, and committed her life to the plight of her people and to the struggle for indigenous rights. And no-one was more inspired by Oodgeroo than Sam Watson.

A high-profile Aboriginal spokesman in Queensland, Watson now teaches a course called Oodgeroo Studies at the University of Queensland. He is also a patron of indigenous arts, part of Link Up, an organisation that reunites people of the Stolen Generation with their kin, and a playwright.

His first play, *The Mack*, was about an Aboriginal family living in Brisbane's West End. Watson says that Aboriginal humour is quite unique, and his play had plenty of it. 'Quite a few of our mob were really impressed,' he says.

His second play, *Oodgeroo: Bloodline to Country*, has just finished a season at Brisbane's La Boite theatre. He considers it one of the most important pieces that he's written. 'She's one of my great heroes. I've read all her speeches. I wanted to acknowledge her contribution to the struggle.'

Although Oodgeroo was a promoter of reconciliation, Watson takes a different line. 'Since 1770 our land was invaded. There was a genocide, with massive destruction of people, land, song, dance and ritual.' He has his doubts about reconciliation – about what it can deliver for his people. Watson is a realist. He's seen the appalling conditions that many of his people endure. He works hard, ever hopeful of change. At times it's an arduous journey.

He's also seen places where a bit of support makes a difference.

He cites Redfern in inner-city Sydney, and South Brisbane as examples; how Catholic parishes in both locations have responded. How they embraced indigenous people. In the case of

Redfern, the parish used to; that is, until the parish priest, named Fr Ted Kennedy, died. Fr Ted was an iconic figure, an agitator for Aboriginal justice. He was a priest who believed that to be Christian required embracing the marginalised, the poor, and the dispossessed. At times as many as 100 Aboriginal people would bed down in his presbytery for the night.

'I knew about St Mary's long before I first went there,' Watson says. He developed a connection with the church through its drop-in centre run for homeless people. And over time the relationship flourished, not only between Watson and the church, but between the Murri (local Aboriginal) people and the church. 'They allowed us to run our services there.'

Watson has a lot of time for Fr Peter Kennedy and Fr Terry Fitzpatrick. He considers Kennedy an important leader. 'Peter and Terry try to take the church to marginalised people, the ones Jesus would have gone to. Our mob feel comfy in the church. Even though our park people come in intoxicated, they don't exclude them.'

He believes Kennedy and Fitzpatrick recognise what's driven people to be in the desperate situation they are in. 'They can connect with these people, and see them as real human beings. They're not aloof.'

Watson particularly liked the portrayal of Kennedy and Fitzpatrick in the opening scene of the documentary about Kennedy on the ABC's *Australian Story*. Kennedy, Fitzpatrick and his son are sitting in the living room watching a TV episode of the British comedy *Father Ted*. Watson liked the way the documentary portrayed the St Mary's priests as real people, with real lives. He finds them both very approachable, extremely down-to-earth.

These days Watson is just as likely to be attending the Sunday service as visiting the drop-in centre. 'I'm not a Christian. I'm a Murri Buddhist, but I feel comfy being part of St Mary's,' he says. His paternal grandmother was a very strict, orthodox Catholic, and he's not sure that she'd be happy with the way things are at St Mary's. He laughs at the thought of it.

'Terry and Peter are important, but in the Aboriginal tradition, everyone in the community has an important part to play.' He thinks it's like that at St Mary's. Changing the location of the church has made little difference to Watson. 'The TLC space has become a very personal sacred space. I draw warmth and empathy from the service.' A man who is often in demand, Watson finds that his participation in the Sunday service provides a way to recharge his spiritual batteries.

He believes people have a lot of respect for each other at St Mary's. 'Like *The Big Issue* fellow. He's always out the front. He's such an integral part of the place . . . And also the positive role played by women.' He adds that from time to time women correct Fitzpatrick and Kennedy, and that's not a bad thing.

When Watson's recent play was on in Brisbane, 200 people from St Mary's went along to see it. That's around one-third of the regular congregation. Watson felt they didn't just go because of him. 'Many of them had met or knew Aunty Kath, so they were keen to go along.'

Terry Fitzpatrick was very moved by the play. He describes how at the end of the performance the audience stood to applaud. He felt it was their way of paying tribute to the woman the play was about, a thank you to the woman she was to so many people. 'They were honouring her poetry, which continues to connect us to the land we are on and to the people who cared for this place for thousands of years,' he says.

Watson's play was on in Brisbane in the lead-up to NAIDOC week – originally *The National Aboriginal and Islanders Day Observance Committee* but which has now become a week-long celebration. That Sunday, Watson stood at the microphone at St Mary's and gave a welcome to country. This is what he said:

'On behalf of the Jagara tribal nation, south of the Brisbane River, and the Turrbal tribal nation, north of the Brisbane River, and other tribal groups all whose land adjoins us here. For instance the Yugamby, Wakka Wakka, Jiniburra and Quandamooka peoples. And the Munnenjarlie people whose land goes back into the mountains behind the Gold Coast and joins the land of the Bundjalung peoples. The river is the gathering point for all Aboriginal people. The river is known as Maiwar. It runs out into the bay known as Quandamooka. We have blood ties for our people with the Nunuccal people from Stradbroke Island. Their land is known as Minjerribah, the place of the Aboriginal Mosquito Dreaming. They had special ceremony and rituals associated with mosquitoes.

'The place where we gather today is known as Kurilpa, the place of the water rat. It is also the living place of Kabul, the giant carpet snake, the rainbow serpent, so sacred to our people.

'For Aboriginal people it is a joy to be with people who also share a high regard for the land, ceremony and ritual. So on behalf of all our mob at this time of year, the first Sunday in July, we celebrate NAIDOC week where we welcome you to our country.

'NAIDOC week launches week-long celebrations to showcase Aboriginal culture and to connect with all peoples right across the country. So on behalf of all my people we welcome you to this place on this very special day.'

On occasions, Watson has given homilies at St Mary's. He has also become an integral part of congregation. Speaking about the treaty that was made between St Mary's and the local indigenous community in 2008, Watson says that it was a launch; that it has strengthened the links. 'It's a work in progress,' he says reflectively. 'Yes, a work in progress.'

MONIQUE NELSON

Monique Nelson was seven years old when she first went to St Mary's. It was the parish her parents chose when they moved to Brisbane. Monique didn't have any say in the church her parents selected, but now at 18 years of age, she's glad it was St Mary's.

Mary Nelson, Monique's mother, met Fr Terry Fitzpatrick when she was teaching in Toowoomba. She'd gone to prayer groups with him. Her subsequent move to Cairns did not end their contact. When she eventually moved with her family to Brisbane, Mary was keen to attend Mass at Fitzpatrick's parish. The fact that it was a 35-minute drive from her home on the north side of the city to South Brisbane failed to quell her enthusiasm.

St Mary's had many adults Mary and her husband, Darryl, could relate to and they felt comfortable with the style of services. It also had plenty of other children for Monique and her older brother, Anthony, to engage with. 'We all liked it,' says Monique with characteristic enthusiasm.

One of Monique's earliest memories of St Mary's was the parish camp. It was the Nelsons' first year in the church and they were eager to participate. As we talk, Monique begins to reel off the number of families they met on that camp who later became good friends. 'There was Michael Kelly and another couple who later had three children . . . They all still go to St Mary's, and they are like family. We know each other very well.'

But the settled way of life that Monique and her parents had imagined eventually changed. In September 2004, Monique suffered a severe brain bleed. It was diagnosed as a brain aneurism.

What started out as a headache and vision difficulty soon became life-threatening. In many first-time cases it is.

Five days in intensive care and two weeks in hospital failed to resolve the problem. The suggestion that she begin radiation treatment was not one the family agreed with. They knew that radiation could have life-changing side effects. They thought there had to be another way. While they sought second and third opinions, Monique says, 'Mum believes in the power of prayer, and she didn't want to rush in. She said that we should wait . . . '

The first attempt at embolisation (blocking or clotting the bleed) was unsuccessful. A year passed. Monique had to rest and deal with the short-term amnesia which accompanied her condition. A year later, the same surgeon tried again. This time with new techniques the result was better. It was not all they had hoped for, but it was a substantial improvement. Six months later, scans revealed that the aneurism had healed completely. Monique was no longer at risk of a bleed.

Monique now has a shunt from her brain to her stomach that helped drain fluid in the original bleed, but it does not interfere with her love of life, or movement, or sport. An avid soccer player, she represented Queensland in the under-19s when she was only 16 years old. Her team went on to win the nationals. Then, in the beginning of 2007, she was selected in the Australian team which toured in the UK and Ireland. 'It was a brilliant experience. It was wonderful to see other parts of the world and to play the sport I love.'

As a goalkeeper she is used to dealing with pressure. But one other factor she has to contend with is the amnesia that accompanied her brain bleed. While these days it has improved, she does not have all the short-term recall she used to. Does it affect her on the soccer field? 'I'm OK apart from remembering the score,' she says with a howling laugh. She's now at university and admits that she can no longer get away with cramming the night before exams. But she thinks that's not such a high price to pay. For a while it felt like she lost her life, and now she has it back.

What has she learnt from her own life experiences? 'I don't worry too much. I realise that life is temporary, and I know how quickly life can be taken away.' She adds: 'I love to laugh, and maintaining a positive approach to life is important. I have learnt that laughter is the best medicine and having a sense of humour, particularly when times get tough, really helps you pull through.' She lives life in the 'now'. She realises the importance of everyday things: sport, her family and her community.

There is little doubt that Monique loves and admires her parents, as well as her brother. They have been through a lot together. 'We are very good friends,' she says, aware that many young adults are not friends with their parents.

Many people from St Mary's also stuck by her. They prayed for her, visited, and comforted Monique and her parents. Since her health scare she's become much closer to many of the congregation at St Mary's. 'It was good to go back there knowing they'd all supported me.'

Her return was accompanied by a wish to become more involved at St Mary's. As a young adult Monique makes it clear that she's at St Mary's-in-Exile because that's where she wants to be. 'I like to think that I am a woman of faith, and I was even before I got sick. Mum and Dad took my brother and me to St Mary's, but it is our decision to stay.'

Mass is a ritual that Monique finds a necessary part of her life. For a time in Year 11, she played soccer on Saturdays and worked on Sunday, so Mass was off her agenda. She was saving for her airfares to play soccer internationally. 'I really missed going to Mass,' she says emphatically.

What is it about St Mary's that suits her? 'The vibe, the surroundings, how relevant it is to today's society – with prayers about the environment.' She likes the priests too. Peter Kennedy's sense of humour, his down-to-earth approach and passion for social justice have all been noted. She particularly revels in the yarns with Fitzpatrick. They are often post-Mass conversations about football. It's a shared passion.

Ted, the fellow who sells *The Big Issue* out the front of the church, is another person Monique regularly chats to. Monique says he's been part of the parish since she's been going there. She considers her couple of minutes' chat to him a great investment. 'He's got such great wisdom.'

Sometimes Monique takes friends along to St Mary's. Once inside the church, she asks them if they can work out who the priest is. 'It takes them a while,' she says. Once she took a friend who had not been baptised even though the friend's father was

Catholic. 'She was concerned about going along to Mass, worried she might be in trouble.' Those worries were soon allayed. 'She thought it was a cool place to be; very laid back.'

So too Kiki, the Sudanese student who has lived with the Nelson family for the last three years. 'Kiki really enjoyed that people at St Mary's could just get up and say whatever prayers they wanted. And although she didn't really understand what had happened lately, she went to the microphone and said that what they were doing was good.'

For Monique St Mary's is the kind of church in which young people feel comfortable. 'St Mary's is just trying to be relevant in the 21st century. I went to a Catholic school but most of my friends who went there don't go to Mass. They feel it's not relevant . . . And women are very involved at St Mary's. That's important.'

Reflecting on recent events at St Mary's, she finds it hard to believe that such an important decision could be made by the Archbishop based on letters to the priest, without talking to the congregation. She believes that the community taking a stand, and so many of the congregation leaving the church building, is very positive. 'I don't have a problem moving to the TLC building. I feel just as Catholic.'

She felt very disappointed one night when listening to ABC radio she heard the Archbishop of Brisbane question what kind of faith the people at St Mary's had. 'I felt really hurt by that. If he knew my story he might think differently,' she says. She doubts she was the only one with this reaction. But she's not going to dwell on it.

Monique may be only 18 but she knows life, sport, her family and her community are precious. That's where she's committing her energy. That's where she wants to be.

CLAIRE MOORE

It's a Friday afternoon in late July. I'm seated in the office of Labor Senator for Queensland, Claire Moore. With little more than 24 hours' notice she has agreed to an interview. She has warned, however, that I may have to wait. I do. It provides the opportunity to look around her office.

The meeting room where I am seated in her Fortitude Valley office, in inner-city Brisbane, could well be a lounge room. The sofas and the cushions are purple, and even the posters on the wall with sayings from *The Women's International League for Peace and Freedom* are printed in purple on a white background. The bookshelves that skirt three of the walls are brimming with contemporary literature. They range from Frank Brennan's book *Acting on Conscience* to stories of outback indigenous communities. On the little ottoman that serves as a table there's a book of Margaret Preston's paintings and the photojournalism book *Picturing Human Rights*. There's also a hatstand full of colourful hats and dilly bags. The only evidence that it is a Senator's office is the stack of Senate Reports lined up along two sides of the bookshelves.

As Chair of the Senate Community Affairs Committee, Claire Moore travels broadly and often. She knows Australia well. Not only the country, but many of its Catholic churches. Come Sunday, regardless of where she is, Moore finds a Mass to attend. And although China is not a country noted for having Catholic churches, she even found one during her travels to Beijing.

When Moore arrives, she introduces herself and sits on the couch with one leg tucked under her, as if she were at home. Her short greying hair frames a rounded face that smacks of Irish ancestry. She is warm, natural and welcoming, and she makes no attempt to hurry through the interview that separates her from her well-earned weekend.

Moore recalls the first time she went to St Mary's. It was 16 years ago. She was looking for a Sunday evening Mass. She set out for the cathedral but none was on offer. The closest service was in South Brisbane, so she made her way there. The Mass she attended had a lovely feel. It was warm, alive and welcoming. At the time the altar at St Mary's was still at the front of the church, and Micah had not yet begun, but it was a church with lovely liturgies that you 'participated in rather than recited by rote'. She soon became a regular.

Moore believes that, like herself, many of the people who go to St Mary's have a traditional Catholic background: they were taught religion by their parents, went to Catholic schools and still attend Mass regularly. Hers is a lineage that is Irish Catholic on the maternal and the paternal side. She also believes that being Catholic is as much a culture as a religion. 'I'll always self-identify as a Catholic,' she says.

Moore grew up in Toowoomba, and for her, family, school, the nuns and church were central to her world. They were also her moral guides. Every evening at 6.30 p.m., her family said the rosary. It was just one of the many religious traditions that became formative in her life.

Although decades now separate her from her childhood religion classes, Moore has no difficulty reciting part of the catechism – 'What is sin? It is turning against God.' She also recalls the holy pictures she glued all over the page for her projects and the religion prizes she won. She could even write *The Lord's Prayer* with all the punctuation and capital letters. She didn't want to lose points by getting the semicolon in the wrong spot. She laughs about it now, and in the midst of the laughter begins a recital, 'Our Father, capital O, capital F, comma, who art in heaven, semicolon.'

Faith has always been important to Moore. She says she has always talked to God and that she has a great respect for and understanding of Mary, The Virgin. Her mother was a great inspiration, not only because of her faith but because when her father had an accident and was no longer able to do much work, her mother took on several part-time jobs to ensure the family had all they needed.

One of those jobs was for the meteorology bureau, taking readings every three hours on equipment that was set up in the backyard. As a teenager, it may have provided an ideal excuse for coming home late some evenings, but it was a job in which Moore, her two sisters and her parents all played their part. The family never spoke party politics at home, but they did talk about local issues. There was an understanding that talk without action was of little value.

After university, Moore joined the public service. She began in Aboriginal Affairs, and then after 12 months transferred to Social Security where she worked in the area of community liaison as an outreach officer. She enjoyed the work, getting out to regional areas, setting up networks and explaining how policy worked. Some of her closest friendships were formed there.

In 1994, she was elected the Branch Secretary of the Community and Public Service Union, and in 2002 she took up the position of Senator for Queensland. As Chair of the Community Affairs Committee she is involved in senate enquiries into health, ageing, indigenous issues and social-welfare payments.

Moore says that her social conscience was roused by the sharing that took place in her family and in particular her mother's participation in the local area. Of her mother Moore says: 'She was very involved in both the family and the community. Quite feisty too.' Moore was also affected by the dismissal of the Whitlam government in 1975, and inspired by some of Paul Keating's speeches, such as the now famous Redfern Speech.

Her life at times can be hectic, so Mass provides a balance. At St Mary's she's found a community she feels she belongs to even though she often goes to other churches. 'My heart is with St Mary's. Spiritually it's where I have my inner well filled up; where I get peace.'

There are many things about St Mary's that appeal to Moore apart from the liturgy: the work of Micah, the diversity, its inclusiveness, the role of women and the way the congregation is often challenged by speakers, homilies or reflections.

She cites a man she refers to as a colourful local identity. He wears big shorts, carries an umbrella, and it's not unusual for him to stroll through the church during Mass. 'No-one stares, they nod and welcome him.' She suspects it's not like this in other churches.

In regard to women preaching, Moore is perplexed about why this is seen by church authorities as a transgression. She fails to see the problem. If it were a question of content, she would understand, but that does not seem to be the official concern.

These days, however, she feels a tinge of guilt when, on occasion, she goes to the cathedral in Brisbane. Her regret is that recent events in relation to St Mary's played out the way they did, and were magnified in the media. Speaking as a member of St Mary's she says: 'It was happening to us, but we didn't have any impact on it.' Her voice is not angry. It's gentle, yet strong.

Moore retains much respect for the Archbishop of Brisbane. However, she also speaks of the pain that many people at St Mary's have endured. 'People who were in St Mary's feel that their church has expelled them. We've grown up in a culture where the way you distance yourself from God is to commit sin. But in this case there was no sin.'

Her image of St Mary's is a church that celebrates togetherness and inclusion, with liturgies and ceremonies based on praising God. However, she feels this was shunned and blackened by church authorities. She's seen a number of people in tears. Tears of pain.

She was amazed by the amount of media coverage. Moore believes many people, not only those inside the church, were interested to see what would happen to St Mary's. And they still are. If churches like St Mary's are forced into exile, she wonders about the future of the Catholic Church, about the approach and level of control by church authorities.

Moore is a woman prepared to speak her mind. In Parliament, following her conscience, she has voted pro-choice. 'I'm pro-choice, I'm not pro-abortion,' she says, lamenting that this point seems to be lost on those who condemn her. It is a stance that has brought her to the attention of Catholic authorities.

As a parliamentarian Moore may be used to attack, but she is frustrated that the same has happened to St Mary's. She feels the pain caused by recent events will take some time to subside. And for some it may never go away. Ever conscious of injustice in the world, of inequity, of the plight of so many vulnerable and disadvantaged people in society, she asks, 'Haven't we got more to worry about as a Church?'

It is now 7 p.m. Darkness has long settled over Brisbane and the mass exodus home from the city has subsided. Moore has been gracious with her time and her thoughts. Before leaving, I step into her office to get a business card. To the left of her desk is a beautiful Aboriginal cross, not with a crucified body on it, but with bright light radiating from the centre. It seems symbolic of the kind of church Moore hopes for: one that appeals to many cultures, radiates outwards, and is life-giving and inspirational.

JOHN FITZ-WALTER

There are some people who inspire us. They are passionate and capable, and they allow us to see the beauty of the world through their eyes.

John Fitz-Walter, who ran primary school art programs, had a friend like that. His name was Kevin Brown. Fitz-Walter remembers one particular morning when Brown, his art supplier, dropped off an order. They stood outside chatting. Brown, looking at the bright blue sky, said he couldn't wait to go flying that afternoon. An avid pilot, Brown, who had once been a priest and flew around his remote, far-flung parish, had been dubbed 'the flying priest'. Fitz-Walter loved Brown's zest for life and his passion.

When news of a light-plane accident appeared on the news that evening, Fitz-Walter didn't pay much attention. Brown flew solo, and the news reported two fatalities. It wasn't until the following morning that he realised his friend, along with another pilot, had died. It was shattering news.

The funeral was at St Mary's, and Fitz-Walter took time off work to attend. He knew he had to be there. Fr Peter Kennedy and Fr Terry Fitzpatrick dressed in casual clothes, mingled with the mourners. Three other priests dressed in albs sat in the pews. Their services were not required. Kennedy, whose only formal vestment was a stole around his neck, led a simple, graceful service.

It was not Fitz-Walter's first encounter with Kennedy. He'd met him 15 years before at a staff retreat at Tamborine Mountain. Kennedy had been one of the facilitators. While Fitz-Walter enjoyed the retreat, at that time he had other things on his mind. Teresa, his wife, was soon to give birth to their first child. That child would be the first of three.

Over the years Fitz-Walter had visited different churches but at Brown's funeral he sensed that St Mary's was different. The simplicity of the service, the atmosphere and even the set-up of the church, with what parishoners like to call the table rather than the altar in the middle of church, captivated Fitz-Walter.

He recalls the first service he attended after the funeral. It was Sunday, early evening. Kennedy and Fitzpatrick were away. With no priests present, women presided over the liturgy and gave out consecrated hosts. He soon discovered that other services had their surprises too – a variety of speakers giving homilies. Before long, St Mary's became a regular part of Fitz-Walter's weekend. Initially he came alone. His wife had given formal Catholicism away. When Fitz-Walter walked into St Mary's church, he was following the footsteps of generations of his own family.

Keeping up with Fitz-Walter as he rattles off stories, intricacies and details of his maternal and paternal lineage is like trying to keep up with a 747 heading down the runway in preparation for take-off.

Fitz-Walter's paternal great-grandparents had individually migrated from Ireland. After marrying in Toowoomba they settled in South Brisbane. Their daughter, May (Margaret Mary), who was Fitz-Walter's grandmother, was born in 1887. A woman of stern faith, she attended the church and the primary school at St Mary's in the 1890s, not long after Mary MacKillop's sisters had departed. Not marrying until she was 32 years of age, rumour has it she was referred to as 'the spinster of Merivale Street'.

In 1919, Fitz-Walter's paternal grandfather, Cecil, married May at St Mary's soon after the outbreak of Spanish flu. The marriage was delayed until the epidemic had passed. While the couple moved to Charleville for some years, May returned with her brood to live at her mother's house just down the road from St Mary's. The church which May and her children – one was Fitz-Walter's father – regularly attended, until they moved, was St Mary's. Given his mother's upbringing in South Brisbane, Fitz-Walter's father often returned to the church, albeit mostly for funerals.

Fitz-Walter's father remembers Christmas at St Mary's in the 1930s. He was about eight years of age when he peered at the nativity scene. There he saw a dark-skinned Jesus. The young boy was shocked. His son, John Fitz-Walter, is amazed by the story. Decades later, in his local parish at Graceville, the parish he belonged to before coming to St Mary's, the parish priest had made a request: that he darken the complexion of the baby Jesus. Fitz-Walter obliged. It was an attempt to present a more realistic image of the Christ child.

After a few months attending Mass at St Mary's, Fitz-Walter was asked to be a greeter. The once-a-month role was to welcome people at the beginning of the liturgy and to invite them to greet one another; to read the opening prayer and acknowledge the traditional owners of the land. After inviting the congregation to bring forward their prayers of the faithful, he would ask people to gather around the table for the Eucharistic celebration. Fitz-Walter accepted; after all, he likes to participate rather than to simply spectate.

Fitz-Walter really appreciates the way the community gathers around the table; the way they all stand together. 'It takes the focus off the priests. The priests are not the pinnacle. They are one of the community . . . It's symbolic of authority being flattened out.'

Fitz-Walter is a reflective fellow with a clear deep voice that would be suited to radio. He has a gentle presence and he knows how to commit himself to the moment. He is passionate about cultivating the fullness of the human spirit, about each of us being so much more than the jobs we do or the money we earn.

He loves art, not so much for the pictures or images it produces, but for the activity or process; for what it draws out of people, how it develops them, how it gets people in touch with emotions, ideas, identity, and spirituality. Life he believes is often lived too narrowly. The gift of art, be it music, dance, drama, media or visual arts, is that 'it can take us out of the small parameters in which we normally live'. It is its openness that he is drawn to. As Fitz-Walter describes what art means to him, there is a sense that he is also describing the type of church he is drawn to: open rather than rigid, deeply spiritual, able to accept and live in the mystery. One that encourages exploration rather than imposition.

Not content to simply be a greeter at St Mary's, Fitz-Walter soon put his artistic talent to work in the church. He began creating crosses, painting scenes and banners. One of those banners was ten metres long. It was for Lent/Easter, and it happened to coincide with the plight of recently arrived asylum seekers and preceded the beginning of the Iraq war. On one side of the banner were images of peace, with women and children. On the other, images of destruction and chaos. In the middle between the two extremities was Uluru, the centre of Australia, beneath a deep star-filled sky and a procession of dispossessed peoples moving towards it, exiled. His art was not separate from reality, but deeply immersed in it.

The notion of being immersed in the world was something Fitz-Walter grew up with. He had an excellent family example. She was a Good Samaritan sister who also happened to be his aunt.

Fitz-Walter describes his aunt as an intelligent woman. He is impressed that she studied in Rome, in a language other than English. She also earned postgraduate degrees. She might well have buried herself in her studies, but instead his aunt opened herself to the world. She saw the homelessness and desperation of people living around inner-city Sydney and knew she had to respond. She told her order she was going to live in a house with another sister, and run a type of halfway house. Before long she was running six houses.

Fitz-Walter recalls spending a day with this Good Samaritan sister around Surry Hills and Redfern in the 1980s. They'd walk along, and people who had seen the hard side of life, who knew her, would stop her in the street, come up and kiss her. 'I was in awe of her,' says Fitz-Walter.

In St Mary's, Fitz-Walter found a church that resonated with his sense of social involvement. He began supporting projects, not just artistically. But what he didn't know was that before long he was going to be on the receiving end of support.

On Saturday 12 August 2006, Fitz-Walter who was an experienced cyclist, headed along a bike path he knew well: the gentle incline down under the Indooroopilly bridge, the curve in the track at the bottom of the hill, and the overgrown grass on the hillside. He'd seen it all before. But what he hadn't seen was the young woman approaching in the opposite direction. Nor had she caught sight of him. Fitz-Walter never glimpsed her until she was right in his path. He swung hard to avoid her, hitting the metal guardrail that separated the road and the bikeway. He went straight through it and landed headfirst on the road.

Fitz-Walter is not able to recall much about the accident, the weeks in hospital, or his time at the Brain Injury Rehabilitation Unit. What he does recall is his dislocated shoulder, the collapsed lung and the brain damage he incurred. It was the latter which has had long-term effects. He has lost the right field of vision in both eyes and he has partial hearing loss.

Since then Fitz-Walter's life has changed dramatically. Full-time work, driving and cycling are just examples of activities which are now outside his can-do list. He is not one to lament; not one for self-pity. But having his vision reduced by around seventy per cent has taken a toll on the person he is, or used to be. And like all transitions, it takes time to adjust.

When news of his accident was announced at St Mary's, the Masses were immediately dedicated to Fitz-Walter's wellbeing and recovery. It was support he really appreciated. But it felt strange to be on the reciprocal side of prayer. 'I much prefer praying for others,' he says. His memory of all the visitors from St Mary's who came to see him is not clear. But he knows they came. And they have continued to support Fitz-Walter and his wife. That support has included bringing around meals – regularly.

Since the accident Fitz-Walter comments that, wife and children aside, St Mary's has been more his family than his own three brothers and his parents, the difference being that he just knew that the community was there for him.

These days Teresa, his wife, often accompanies Fitz-Walter to Mass. She's a dynamic woman. She took him out of the rehabilitation unit when, weeks after the accident, she found him lying motionless in the foetal position in bed. She knew that he needed to be with his family. And Teresa provided so much care.

It has been a dramatic change for the family. Fitz-Walter particularly feels the effect it has had on his children. On the odd occasion he grieves his own loss; the loss of visual quantity and clear detailed sight; the loss of independence.

Lake Cootharaba, north of Noosa Heads, is one of Fitz-Walter's favourite places. He used to go there on camping trips with his son and a few friends. It is a precious place he has etched in his memory: its breadth, expansiveness, clear untainted skies, and waters that teem with flickering, dancing, speckled light. When, after the accident, he returned, he looked across the lake, but his vista was narrowed. It was filled with granular misty and shadowy darkness. It lacked cleanness, clarity, contrast and defined colour. Internally he howled at the grim reality of it.

Fitz-Walter would not deny that he has been through difficult times, but he is getting on with his life. He is now back at work one and a half days a week and he is actively involved in his church community. It is where he belongs. Many at St Mary's consider him an inspiration. But most of all they enjoy his company, his humour, his gentle presence and his insightful way of seeing the world.

ESSAYS AND
REFLECTIONS

CREATION OR DESTRUCTION?

by Frances Devlin-Glass

For the first time in several decades, the place of the Catholic Church in the world – what it is and who it's for, how it worships and thinks, and its mission in the world – is being passionately debated outside the cloisters. The parishioners of St Mary's, South Brisbane, are in debate, a multi-vocal affair, with their archbishop (John Bathersby) and priest (Fr Peter Kennedy). Whether this is creating, as the proponents for Peter Kennedy argue, a viable 21st-century version of Catholicism, or is a legitimate exercise in power and a reassertion of orthodox theology and liturgy by the hierarchy, is contested. Whether the matter of Peter Kennedy's 'insubordination' can be easily separated from the intentions to remain in the Catholic communion by many of his parishioners is also as yet somewhat unclear. But the issue has raised some compelling debate about the nature of Christian commitment in the 21st century, and whether or not theology and social justice are mutually exclusive.

History and geography of St Mary's

St Mary's, according to its historian/archivist, Maggie Boyle (who is also a parishioner), is one of the oldest parishes in the city of Brisbane. The New South Wales Department of Public Works gazetted a grant of land for a Roman Catholic church in 1858, a year before Queensland became a separate colony. By 1866, there was a functioning church and school, run by the Mercy nuns.

When Mary MacKillop (Australian-born of Scots parents) brought her new Australian order, the Sisters of St Joseph, to

Brisbane in 1870, they were offered the school and it ran for a decade. Mary MacKillop lived and worked in South Brisbane for fifteen months. Her mission was to the poor and marginalised, and she was to go on to bring education to the outback and to Aborigines. She withdrew her nuns from this part of Queensland after a falling-out with Irish-born Bishop James Quinn, over whether her sisters lived by the rules they had devised, or whether the Bishop had a right to impose his rules.

South Brisbane became a bustling quayside town with an industrial and commercial focus in the 1880s: 25 000 people lived in South Brisbane in 1888 and the railway had finally arrived in 1884, providing more lowly paid work. By 1893, a new church had been built and the Mercy nuns resumed their work in the school and old church buildings, expanding again in 1909. They built a convent in South Brisbane in 1915, thereby avoiding the need to travel backwards and forwards to All Hallows across the river.

The higher ground around Highgate Hill was taken by the elites of Brisbane, and working-class people settled on the flats on a flood-prone section of the mighty Brisbane River. It was not a desirable place to live. The river flooded catastrophically in 1893, removing the main bridge linking South Brisbane to the administrative centre of town, north of the river, and doing serious damage in the lower parts of Stanley Street. This only slowed development but South Brisbane by then was a hub for rail traffic, with a flour mill, dry docks, and meat works.

One of the earliest curates was an Irish priest, Fr Paul Keating, who boasted a BA from Queen's College, Dublin, an unusual qualification for the period. He was at St Mary's for only seven months, dying of pneumonic influenza in 1919, aged one day short of 26. In that short time, he was active in setting up the first Catholic college, St Leo's, at the University of Queensland (originally on Wickham Terrace).

As the suburbs of Brisbane developed, and the centre of shipping moved from South Brisbane to downstream of the Story Bridge at Newstead and Hamilton after 1940, and the railway yards closed, the original lowly paid workers moved out, and the cheap, lower parts of the suburb became home successively to waves of migrants after the post-WWII boom. St Mary's became a focus for waves of Polish, Dutch, Lithuanians and Slovenians. South Brisbane was fast becoming an industrial slum, but was still home to the poor. The inclusive credentials of St Mary's are deep. Lebanese Christians (David Malouf grew up in the area), ministered to by Fr Khoury, worshipped there until they built their own church in 1935, and successive waves of European migrants came to the church in the early 1950s. However, numbers at the school declined. It closed in 1964, and the convent soon after in 1968. The last parish priest left in 1980, the congregation having shrunk to just 50. St Mary's had lost its status as a parish.

In 1980, Fr Peter Kennedy was appointed prison chaplain to the nearby Boggo Road jail (he also had responsibility for all the jails in south-east Queensland) and Administrator of St Mary's, now demoted from a parish to a Mass Centre. Peter Kennedy's social justice credentials, and those of the St Mary's community, are unquestioned by those opposed to him. As prison chaplain, he recognised that he alone could not meet the needs of prisoners and encouraged the community to participate in the development of Catholic Prison Ministry which still operates today under the auspices of Centacare. He concerned himself not just with prison visits, but also with educating prisoners, and worrying about what happened to them on release. Their practical needs for shelter, food and work, and their education while in jail, were part of their rehabilitation as far as he was concerned. Kennedy was able to inspire and foster new thinking about how their needs and those of their families were met.

In 1987, Peter Kennedy built a spirituality centre in the Numinbah Valley, in the hills behind the Gold Coast. He continued to hold church services at St Mary's on Sundays, and attendances increased. Attendees often did not live locally but were drawn by the challenge of his form of witness – by his particular variety of Catholic social action and social-justice agendas. At St Mary's Church, many homeless, indigenous and mentally ill people used to share the space routinely with parishioners at Mass. His followers talk of acts of kindness, like bringing the drunk, mentally disturbed, or vagrant into the church, thereby encouraging his middle-class parishioners to interact with such people. A 'Gathering Day' was held in 1989 and a Leadership Team was established by 1995, employing part-time liturgy and community workers. Numbers attending these services swelled to 800 people.

In 1993, the Jubilee Year of St Mary's, community members initiated and committed 10 per cent of parish income to establish a collective response to social justice and Micah Projects Inc. was formed as a local, not-for-profit organisation in 1995. With the outsourcing of social services by government, it concerns itself with homelessness, support for young parents, mental health and disability, and abuse in faith communities and church and state run institutions. In 10 years, the Esther Center, an activity of Micah Projects, has responded to 3000 complaints about abuse by clergy, and by people in church and state-run institutions. By 1998, Micah Projects Incorporated was run on professional lines, attracting grants from government and other sources, and working in a variety of social-welfare initiatives.

Nearby Musgrave Park has been an unofficial 'home' to Aboriginal people. Dennis Walker, son of Oodgeroo Noonuccal, initiated a Sacred Treaty Circle and was given space for an icon in the church grounds. A treaty was signed on 30 November 2008, though the legality of the 'treaty' is debated by some. It is this openness to all comers that perhaps attracts today's more middle-class and better-educated parishioner.

Peter Kennedy, sincerely believing he is doing what Pope Benedict enjoined, 'everyone has a place in the Church', openly attends gay unions (though does not solemnise them) and welcomes Rainbow coalition activists into his church, though it is ironic that many gay men prefer the more traditional 'bells and smells' and frocks on offer at the Cathedral church. His tolerance and support for such people is, of course, unwelcome to those such as Cardinal George Pell who has actively refused, and requires his priests to refuse, communion to people flaunting their gay preferences. Kennedy's supporters protest that this is untheological, that only God can make such discriminations.

The other group that the church, in the eras of John Paul II and Benedict, marginalises, but must increasingly draw on for minor sacramental function (for distributing communion, taking communion to the ill etc.), is women. Much is made by Kennedy's opponents that he allows women to 'preach'. Homilies by women with something to say, of course, are not an unfamiliar phenomenon in many Catholic churches around Australia, but it is noted in South Brisbane.

The role of vigilantes

Since 1980, the liturgy had evolved and these changes were welcomed by many, but not by all. Groups of right-wing Catholics (Richard Stokes is their spokesman in Brisbane, but see their site, Stones Will Shout, and their Newsletter, Into the Deep, www.stoneswillshout.com, for a sense of their model of church), usually those who have severe misgivings about Vatican II, have been organising for a decade to collect evidence, in churches around Australia, of practices of which they disapprove, and sending reports to Rome. Archbishop Bathersby has been seeking change at St Mary's since 2004, and similar events to what has transpired at St Mary's have been continually occurring in other Brisbane parishes since the mid-1980s (e.g. the public censuring of Fr Bill O'Shea, Bishop John Gerry's public and private humiliation for his support of the decriminalisation of homosexuality in Queensland, though he was careful not to endorse the practices). Fr Kennedy's easy social relations, his sureness (some might say cockiness) about his ministry, and his willingness to seek publicity for what he sees as a prophetic mission and, on the other side, his opposite number's avoidance of it and lack of media savvy have helped to create an atmosphere in which mutual respect cannot be guaranteed. Headlines shout: 'Defiant priest plans Mass after sacking' and 'A Church collapsing without foundations'.

The reports sent to Rome by the vigilantes tend to be edited versions of liturgical forms and expressions of theology, and visual data – video clips of liturgy, and photographs, for example, of the alleged Buddha in the church at St Mary's (Kennedy argues it is a statue of a monk praying, and not the Buddha, and has a place in the church as an ecumenical gesture towards the Buddhist group that has met there for 10 years on Monday evenings). The issue of the statue seems to be more Stokes's concern than the Archbishop's who was recently feted by Rome and the Australian government for his ecumenism.

Kennedy is accused of:

- allowing priest *and people* to speak the words of consecration at Mass (instead of the priest speaking the words alone); allowing women to preach; not using vestments at Mass;
- using a gender-inclusive language ('In the name of the Creator, the Redeemer and the Sanctifier') for baptisms (thereby invalidating the baptisms of many children and adults);

- soft-pedalling the divinity of Jesus in his liturgies; and expressing his doubts about such matters as Virgin birth to the media, though he is not accused of preaching this within his church;
and
- indoctrinating his flock by making social justice the key issue in his preaching.

It seems Kennedy may be less interested in theology than in social justice, and the debate with him may be Stokes's more than Bathersby's. Questions raised by the vigilantes' actions include: are the two ways of being in the Church mutually exclusive? How central is dogma, theology and set liturgical forms in the life of the Church, and how are experiments/deviations to be permitted or managed/punished? Is any experimentation with liturgy tolerated/tolerable?

The media have played up the drama and dumbed down the nuances, and no doubt thrown accelerant on a debate that would normally be private in the parish. The debate as the media and the hierarchy portray it is heavily polarised. The voices on the far right of Australian politics, Christopher Pearson, Andrew Bolt and others, have weighed in, in *The Australian*, predictably against the pro-Kennedy faction. Christopher Pearson sneeringly mocks 'cafeteria' Catholicism – selective adherence to those aspects of faith which are congenial and ignoring the rest. Perhaps the most useful aspect of the debate is the revivification of such debates and the owning of them by parishioners.

Parishioners' concerns

Those parishioners I have spoken to reveal a broad spectrum of support, and intelligent critique, of Peter Kennedy. Some are worried, even anguished, about the prospect (threatened) of being considered 'out of communion with Rome' when they believe they belong; others are incensed that the media stoush has derailed the 'real' issues of their spiritual lives at St Mary's. More than one expressed disquiet at the phenomenon of the 'celebrity priest' and worried that guru-status had been conferred on Kennedy, and that without him the movement would be unsustainable. There is real debate among the ordinary parishioners about how similar or different the forms of worship actually are to more traditional forms of Catholic liturgy. One expressed concern about St Mary's becoming a Catholic-inflected Hillsong, a liturgical 'circus', and worries about the legitimacy of reviving 1970s excitement, especially by remobilising songs like 'We Shall Not Be Moved'. That such Catholics can be committed and also qualify their support is important in such a debate, but such modulation is not necessarily shared by all three parties to the dispute. The situation in which the Church finds itself is very different from that pertaining at the time of Vatican Council II when so many parishioners were under-educated and inclined to accept uncritically ecclesiastical authority. The St Mary's parishioners are aware of power and its operations, gender-conscious, and more accepting of sexual, racial and cultural difference, and aware of the Church's role in institutionalising pathological inequities. They are as educated, often more so than some of their pastors. Some of the best commentary I've read on what is at issue liturgically is the thoughtful blog from ex-parishioner and religious studies academic, Michael Carden, who addresses the liturgical issues critically (see http://michaelcardensjottings. blogspot.com/2009/02/election-time-in-queensland.html).

Nor does the power differential between hierarchy and so-called maverick priest help the matter. Not that Fr Kennedy is alone in preaching an Australian version of 'liberation theology' and social justice, and increasingly those priests who align with him are speaking out. The risk is, of course, to their livelihoods (they are professional pastors who do not want to be sacked) and to their parishes (who do not want to lose them), if they do speak out. How many priests can Australian dioceses afford to lose? What are the implications in terms of closeness to their parishes of bringing in, as is happening, priests from the Philippines and Africa, however well-trained? Is this form of reverse colonialism similar to or different from the mass importation of priests and nuns from Ireland in the 19th and early 20th centuries? These are complex issues of power and neo-colonialism, and culture, and it seems to me that how the hierarchy manages this symptomatic event is crucial. What is the price of change in the Catholic Church?

Showdown
The self-styled vigilantes' complaints to Rome have in the last two papacies gained traction, and the local Archbishop (also the

target of their complaints), John Bathersby, could no longer avoid taking action against a person who was and is, tragically, no longer a close friend. The two men have confronted each other, but the Archbishop, rather than meeting with the parishioners, has conducted his business by letter. The threat in a letter in March 2008 to the congregation, of not only sacking Peter Kennedy but excommunicating those who follow him, was received by parishioners with disquiet. In an attempt to calm the situation, mediation was mooted, but the choice of Ian Callinan, the former SC and High Court Judge with known conservative tendencies, was not acceptable to Fr Kennedy. Again, by letter, Kennedy was formally sacked and ordered to surrender the keys of the church to Dean Howell, the successor determined by the Archbishop on 21 February 2009. He resisted. A formal process of negotiation, but not mediation as the terms were not mutually agreed upon, eventually took place with the Parish Council on 27 March 2009, in the absence of both Fr Kennedy and the Archbishop. The 'agreement' reached with representatives of the parish was that the keys were relinquished, and the Archbishop's representative, the Dean of St Stephen's Cathedral, took over on 20 April 2009.

Peter Kennedy and his supporters established a 'church in exile' at the Trades Hall and Micah Projects Ltd moved out of the parish house at the end of June. About 70 people currently worship at St Mary's and 750 at St Mary's-in-Exile. The parishioners have voted with their feet.

The author warmly thanks Maggie Boyle for her archival research and timeline of the parish and its development from 1858 to the present.

Frances Devlin-Glass (Honorary Associate Professor, Deakin University) is a retired academic, and currently an editor of the online Journal of the Association for Australian Literature (JASAL), the Australasian Journal for Irish Studies, and on the editorial board of the Australian Irish Heritage Network's magazine, Tinteán. She has also been foundation director of Bloomsday in Melbourne since 1994.

CHRISTIANITY CONFRONTS ITS GREATEST CHALLENGE

by Michael Morwood

The events in St Mary's, South Brisbane, can too readily be dismissed as an in-house Roman Catholic dispute culminating in the Archbishop removing a priest he considers to be unfaithful to Roman Catholic teaching and practice.

This dispute is more far-reaching than that. What we see here is not so much the tip of an iceberg but rather the flaring of a volcano. This volcano has enormous size and power. Institutional Christianity would do well to deal with it rather than plug holes.

What does this volcano represent and why does institutional Christianity, all the while proclaiming that 'the truth will set you free', steadfastly and even dishonestly refuse to engage the issues?

The refusal to engage has an uncanny resemblance to the refusal to engage Galileo.

Scientific knowledge clashed with Scripture and belief set in concrete. Far easier to silence (try to plug the volcano erupting) the source of knowledge rather than confront issues that called long-cherished beliefs and Church authority into question. It took the Roman Catholic Church centuries to apologise for its treatment of Galileo. And once again, Church authority is digging in the heels and refusing to engage what is staring them in the face.

The fundamental issue today is also scientific. One example is the Hubble Telescope and its pictures that reveal to us a universe we could never have imagined even 25 years ago – a universe with hundreds of billions of galaxies, each with hundreds of billions of stars. Another example is 20th-century knowledge about the age of this planet and how life developed on it.

This scientific 'story' not only invites but demands that Christians (and people of all religions) reflect on their understanding of the mystery they call 'God' in this context. Christianity traditionally has two streams of thought.

One stream of thought proclaims that God is everywhere as the source and sustainer of all that is. In this thinking everyone and everything is connected in and through this Presence. And, as some great Christian thinkers have told us very clearly, this Presence is beyond our comprehension, our understanding and our human images. This needs to be clearly understood. This is part of traditional Christian thinking. It is basic Christianity.

The other stream of thought has focused on God as a deity who thinks, plots, plans, reacts, intervenes and plays favourites. In simple terms, this deity can be referred to as the 'elsewhere God' because he denied access to himself and then sent 'his Son' (from where?) to earth.

Jesus, in the first stream of thought, is the revealer of God-with-us (everyone!) in our living and loving. He opens eyes and minds to the unseen reality in which we are all immersed and have existence. Jesus challenged people to give expression to this Presence in their lives, so that the 'reign' of God, characterised by compassion, generosity, forgiveness and love, would be evident among us.

In the second stream of thought, developed in the Christian Scriptures well after Jesus died, Jesus became the unique 'way' to the elsewhere deity. He 'opened the gates of heaven'; he 'saved' us. Or, at least, he 'saved' people who believed he was the unique way to God.

It is not surprising that the second stream of thinking about God and Jesus came to dominate the Christian religion. After the break with its mother religion, Judaism, the Christian Church claimed to have unique access to God through Jesus.

As Cicero would ask, 'Who gained?'

Clearly institutional Christianity had much to gain by this thinking. It gave the new religion unique identity and authority. It could – and did – claim that only through entrance into this Church and fidelity to its beliefs could anyone have access to God when they died.

The Christian religion, in its creedal statements, locked itself into this story of Jesus gaining access to an elsewhere deity rather than honouring Jesus' preaching about God-with-us. Its statements about the 'divinity' of Jesus are encased in this dualistic notion of a God who lives somewhere else and only someone on God's side, as it were, could mend the disconnection between heaven and earth. So Jesus has to be radically different from the rest of humankind. But what if there were no disconnection in the first place? Catholic theologians are not allowed to publicly discuss the ramifications of such thinking.

The Catholic Church in its sacramental system is also locked into a theological worldview of the sacred/God essentially existing elsewhere and the need for men with special powers, using just the right and proper words and gestures to access that Presence and mediate it to a dependent laity. Fr Kennedy, it is claimed, did not use the correct, official formula for Baptisms, so now the charge is that the Baptisms may be invalid. For 'invalid' read, 'it does not work'. If Baptism is fundamentally a ritual celebrating a sacred presence and calling people to give witness to that presence in their lives, 'invalid' and 'does not work' are meaningless. They are only meaningful in a theological worldview that claims to have access to the divine, along with claims of having a unique formula to make the divine 'come'.

And now this religion is facing the biggest shift ever in its history because so many Christians simply no longer give credence to the worldview or the notion of God that underpins traditional, acceptable, orthodox Christian theology and a great deal of Catholic sacramental practice.These Christians are not being 'unfaithful' to Jesus or the God Jesus preached or a stream of thought that has always been part of Christian thinking. They just want their religion to shift from a no-longer-believable story about or emphasis on a deity who has definite opinions on whether women should be ordained priests or stem cell research or whatever. They want their religion to honour God's presence in people the way Jesus did. They want prayer and liturgy to reflect this Presence with them and to be empowered by it rather than constantly reaching out to a listening deity who might or might not hear or answer their prayers. They want their religion to preach what Jesus preached: the accessibility of the Divine Presence to all people who reflect on their love and generosity.

But, in the Roman Catholic Church, Rome and Episcopal authority do not want this to happen. It seems there is intense fear that the Christian religion will collapse and lose its identity; central authority (and power) will be eroded if there is any shift from thinking about Jesus as the unique 'way' to an elsewhere God. So there exists this tight control, this constant plugging of holes to stop the volcano erupting. Theologians are silenced to such an extent that there now exists in the Roman Catholic Church what can only be called a climate of acute intellectual dishonesty, driven by Rome and many bishops. Theologians can not say or write what they really think about this enormous shift and its implications for the Christian Creed and Church identity because they will be silenced. Catholic parishes have been under enormous pressure for some years, with a watchdog, reporting mentality rife in some dioceses, not to make changes to rituals, even though the rituals are shot through with notions of and language about an elsewhere deity.

Sadly, the expression given to this shift in St Mary's, South Brisbane, has been officially plugged. This has been done in the name of fidelity to Church doctrine and practice. The Archbishop may well think he had right on his side as well as absolute power and authority. But that's what happened with Galileo and the greatest disappointment for anyone with any understanding of the real issues at stake in this dispute is that Church authority figures are looking at 'truth' with blinkers on. There is another 'story' about God and the universe, about Jesus as revealer of that Mystery, about the Church doing faithfully what Jesus did. It's a wonderful story, faithful to Christian roots, and it has the potential to revitalise the Church at all levels. Rome says Catholics are not allowed to tell, preach or celebrate this story in any shape or form. The Archbishop does what Rome tells him to do – an all too familiar story all around the world in recent years.

Christianity and the Roman Catholic Church need to be more courageous in facing the world and these times than this.

Michael Morwood, a former Catholic priest, has 40 years experience in retreat, education, parish and adult faith education ministries in Australia. For the past ten years he has lectured extensively in the USA, Canada and Ireland.

His book, From Sand to Solid Ground. Questions of Faith for Modern Christians, *won a USA Catholic Press Award in 2008. His latest book,* Children Praying a New Story, *is a 'Resource for Parents, Grandparents and Teachers' wanting to nurture future generations in a faith perspective grounded in a contemporary understanding of the universe.*

Michael is the Associate Director of Adult Spiritual Renewal & Empowerment, Inc.

FIGHT OR FLIGHT

by Bronwyn Lay

In *Mad Max: The Road Warrior* Mel Gibson sits on a plank of wood, leans against some decrepit tyres and stares down at the ragamuffin community under siege from big men with weird weapons. As they squabble about survival tactics, his laconic twang catches their attention, 'You want to get out of here, you talk to me.' After years of hearing Catholics say to each other 'the church is not a democracy' or 'you're only a census catholic' or 'there's no such thing as a cultural catholic, either you are in or out' or 'watch your words, people died so you could critise the Catholic Church' or the best one to use on those of Irish stock, 'you want to do what you want? Then go join Protestants', the idea of Mad Max turning up at the church door is a perfectly suitable escape fantasy.

Born into a Catholic heritage and growing up after the Second Vatican Council meant being surrounded by all sorts of Catholics and, as children are apt to do, I observed the adults with watchful eyes. Mum, drawing on the wisdom of St Therese of Lisieux, used to say that there are many flowers in the church, so I was taken on a tour of the garden and exposed to varieties of Catholics, from the heritage to the hybrids.

The first church I attended was a wooden shack hidden in the bush where a radical priest presided while altar boys picked their noses and parents picked lice from the toddlers' heads. I have attended many masses since: in 1970s architecturally experimental churches where pews circled the altar like petals and electric guitars rocked the foundations; sitting on concrete under a corrugated-iron roof in the Tiwi Islands as stray dogs threatened to join in the longest sign of peace where embracing uncles, aunts, brothers, sisters and cousins left no-one untouched; in football stadiums with thousands who roared when seventy men in frocks paraded across the stage, then descended into miraculous, multicultural silence as the service commenced; in a humble church under the commission flats on Mother's Day where a tired woman gave the sermon as children played at her feet; on a dark evening when a drunk burst through the doors at communion and, before his grubby hands got hold of the eucharistic wine, men in suits whisked him away; in a broken boarding house where elderly homeless men wandered around the kitchen table muttering through their gums as the priest split the reclaimed Tip Top bread and made it sacred; in suburban lounge rooms where a flat screen stared down at the makeshift altar; in the forecourt of the Vatican where piles of penguin nuns elbowed their way to the front; in cathedrals where our forebears echoed through the Latin as the priest turned his back and the stones of the church melted with the glorious sounds of choirboys; sitting in pews next to lesbians who bowed their heads, quietly cried and then went to communion; on the red dirt in Broome on Ash Wednesday where we shared the smoking ceremony of the indigenous peoples and listened to the blessings of both the priest and the local elders in equal measure; in a small village where the struggling African priest was abused mid-sermon by the local French mayor for speaking pathetic French then told to go back to where he came from; and a few weeks before Christmas where a church full of mothers bowed their heads in hopeless solemnity when Van Nguyen faced foreign death gallows at the same time as the priest's shaking hands raised the Eucharist. Sanctioned or unsanctioned, I have been to many Masses and seen that there are many ways to be in the Catholic Church.

But even as a child I realised that often these diverse flowers in the Catholic Church sometimes didn't like each other very much. From behind couches at adult get-togethers and over cups of tea in the church car park there was a lot of laughter and the sharing of lives but I observed moments when the left-wingers call the right-wingers soulless cold money-makers and the right-wingers call the left-wingers heretical humanists with no faith. The rock and roll happy clappers were called superficial and the smells and bells Latin lovers were labelled too serious.

Zigzagging between them all for many years, watching them sporadically persecute and prosecute each other with cold, quiet judgment and open squabbles I learnt this was part of an ongoing story of how hard Catholics can be on each other, which is unsurprising considering that absolute truths loom over their shoulders and God is on everyone's side. This discord was a mere paper cut compared to when the DLP split families and parishes, and totally incomparable to the bloody struggles that raged for centuries in Europe, South America and elsewhere, but as a child I witnessed that, more often than not, the divisions and hard convictions seemed to be made of sand. I'd watch in awe as people in vehement disagreement would shake hands at the sign of peace and head towards the great equalising force of the Eucharist. The child finds solace in watching the miracle of adults finding a way to be together.

To remain a Catholic as an adult requires conviction and constantly walking the balance between substantive and formal justice, doctrinal dictates and personal moral commitments, obedience and freedom, faith and emptiness, legality and mystery, as well as having to constantly rub shoulders with one's nemesis. Catholics, like one-eyed Collingwood supporters, despite being large diverse communities, still have fixed boundaries about who is in and who is out and these kinds of communities can, often unintentionally, force people to quietly start hiding the bits that spill, the bits that, if revealed, risk being excluded. It is very easy in cultures like this to move our struggles into the shadows, but my generation knows all too well that this tactic can have dangerous consequences.

Commitment to the Catholic Church and the life it demands cannot exist without at least a theoretical commitment to love, because as Catholics we are reminded all the time that the man up there on the cross did just that. He loved until they killed him and that kind of love demands everything from you; tragically it can even demand long-held principles. It is understandable that in an awful choice between doctrine and love, between justice and love, between power and love, that love loses out because love is hard to pin down and can't be told to sit still in dogmatic boxes. Battles between the institutional church and those on the ground whose faith has led them to question rules and regulations, exclusions and rituals, are common and have been going on since Adam and could easily continue until Armageddon. Looking back from the safety of adulthood, amidst the Catholic swirl of love, laughter, shared grief and community there was a slim side road which led into the dark forest of religious madness and it seemed to be paved with tiles of justice, doctrine and good intentions. When faced with the decision to follow – to heed inherited wisdom, to toe the party line, to subsume personal ideals into the greater body of doctrine – some find themselves at the fork in the road marked fight or flight as the ominous strains of a steel string guitar filter through the dust.

Standing at the fork in the road with the institutional church looming above in all its finery, Australians might take a moment to look at their own culture. We have a two-hundred-year history of the great transcendental failure where a small mob holds up their palms against the rock-solid shadow of institutional power. Mad Max spoke to us about our tradition to fail gloriously against an unstoppable opponent as the ultimate proof of heroism and Australians pride themselves on giving a hopeless task, like Gallipoli, our best shot. Sometimes, in the face of authority we let ourselves be told what to do for longer than we like, then we snap. We generally don't take up arms, but silently stick two fingers in the air and move off. At this fork in the road some people, very quietly, when no-one is looking, wander off down the road marked flight. It's not dramatic: they meander, pause a bit, look back, consider the options again, then keep on wandering to see what's around the corner, taking slow incremental flight out into God's big church: the world.

In the rare moments we exalt as the norm, like Eureka stockade and Ned Kelly, Australians have been known to stand and fight. History tells us that we fail, but we hope to find redemption in the battle itself. For Catholics it echoes with some of the readings we heard at Mass. As a child I watched adults fight the Catholic Church for not being doctrinal enough; others fought long hard battles to change Church doctrine so that it matched the social realities of our times. Some of these warriors succumbed to madness, bitterness and grief because to take on the Catholic Church requires the resilience of a pit bull and the confidence of a young David. To fight is brave, admirable, but also potentially spiritually suicidal.

The outsider's perspective can shine a different light on what we take for granted. Mahfouz's novel *The Children of Our Alley* followed the trials and tribulations of the children of Abraham and when the figure of Jesus Christ appeared he was portrayed as a wise lunatic who preached love and did insane things like hang out on the fringes, reject power and ask hard questions. To Mahfouz, Jesus was a lovely lunatic, a transcendental failure, because to many who have not been raised in the tradition or felt its power, the idea of Christian love is lunacy. For those who are only trying to live what they believe, to be told you don't belong in the Catholic Church because you have tried to love, lived on the fringes, rejected power and asked hard questions can be confusing. If you love, in a truly radical way, you are asking for trouble inside and outside the institution and saints have been making trouble for the Catholic Church for centuries, but so too have lunatics.

Those who stand and fight the Catholic Church may have a few saints and martyrs on their sides, but this is no guarantee of victory. In *A Few Good Men* Jack Nicholson personified the voice of established practices when he glared across the courtroom at the justice-loving lawyer played by Tom Cruise. Catholics everywhere can hear the truth of his admission when, under the hammer of vicious cross-examination, Nicholson's eyebrows crouched and he thundered, 'You can't handle the truth.' Communities and individuals fighting the Catholic Church may hear the voice of established practices, hard-won doctrine and years of accumulated knowledge boom over the sea from Rome. The voice of institutional power, with centuries of experience at its back, can be very scary and very stubborn and, despite the fuzzy feeling a Hollywood script can deliver, holding onto their construction of the truth is how institutions survive.

The term lapsed Catholic implies that one just forgot to be catholic which, for anyone who has been part of a Catholic community, is impossible. For many there is no veil-tearing moment where faith falls apart and everything meaningful suddenly reveals itself to be nothing, but rather a process of slow incremental flight. To the Jack Nicholsons of the Catholic hierarchy many take their cue from *The Road Warrior* as flight provides an option out of a hopeless battle where bullets of bitterness and frustration can spray willy-nilly. Many Catholics don't take to the desert in a decrepit Kingswood, but embark on a quieter form of flight; hanging around the fringes of the church, which is a lovely place full of interesting people having a laugh, living and dying and trying hard to live what they believe. Some state their case, then slowly walk to the back pews, giving up the fight so they can direct their energies towards working for the sake of greater justice, giving up all they have built within the Church to turn their labour over to God's Big Church. In the back stalls of churches are many who have shaved close to the centre of the institutional church, lived in its shadow and have first-hand experience of what a difficult place it is to inhabit. And over time these people silently build an empire of quiet Christian love that holds parishes and communities together.

Many remain for the smells and bells, the rituals that Catholics hold so dear. Whatever the breadth of the distance between those taking flight and the institutional Church, the wafting smells and ringing of bells might make them yearn for the possibility of transcendence, for the possibility of being embraced by something bigger than their small selves, because a Catholic background imparts a respect for the importance of contemplation and ritual. Without them the world can be a hurly-burly, hot and cold place. Even after taking flight many respect the need for rituals that speak to something deep in our DNA, that connect us to something greater than ourselves, that remind us that we are mere ants in a baffling cosmos and communal, age-old rituals can give us this. That is why the hardened long-gone Catholic can accidentally attend Mass and end up in tears, because they may have experienced that a world without contemplation and ritual can be an individualistic, pathologically lonely place, but they may equally know that a world solely constructed of smells and bells can devour an individual's soul.

There is no doubt that life out in God's big Church is as confronting, spiritually challenging and as existentially difficult as inside God's small church, but many find themselves out there, ironically following what is at the heart of many liturgies, that in the end God is love. Naturally Catholics will undoubtedly continue to make the world a better and worse place just like all churches do in their various ways, but for many of the Catholics who have slowly wandered away, it would be nice to look back and see that those they left on familiar shores were being gentle with each other, because there are so many quiet saints living on those shores, from the Vatican to the shanty towns.

There is another history etched deeper into this land and Vincent Lingiari is one its heroes. In the face of appalling work conditions and the unjust taking of his people's land, the indigenous elder Mr Lingiari walked off the mainstage into a creek bed. He and his people fought without raising arms but by waiting and speaking quiet truths and it took eight years before a tall man poured a handful of sand through his patient hands and justice was done. Flight, in all its guises, might initially look like failure but perhaps it is a brave grab at honesty and survival. If belief in Christian love survives, then those in flight can travel to all corners of the world: to the margins and the centre, to the institutions and to the rebels, and might look back to see that the Catholic Church is capable of change, perhaps not now, but one day and probably in slow incremental ways. They might look back and see, like Mr Lingiari, there is a whole mob of Catholics sitting in circles at the crossroads having a quiet word in an ear here and an ear there, because to walk away means to lose something sacred and they know how to wait.

Bronwyn Lay lives with her family in rural France. She is enrolled in a Masters of English Literature at the University of Geneva and is working on her first novel. Previously she worked as a legal-aid lawyer in Australia with postgraduate qualifications in political theory.

Translation by John Bowden

'IF OBAMA WERE POPE'

by Hans Kung

President Barack Obama has succeeded in a short time in leading the United States out of a mood of despondency and a back-up of reforms, presenting a credible vision of hope and introducing a strategic shift in the domestic and foreign policy of this great country.

In the Catholic Church things are different. The mood is oppressive, the pile-up of reforms paralysing. After his almost four years in office many people see Pope Benedict XVI as another George W. Bush. It is no coincidence that the Pope celebrated his 81st birthday in the White House. Both Bush and Ratzinger are unteachable in matters of birth control and abortion, disinclined to implement any serious reforms, arrogant and without transparency in the way in which they exercise their office, restricting freedoms and human rights.

Like Bush in his time Pope Benedict, too, is suffering from an increasing lack of trust. Many Catholics no longer expect anything of him. Even worse, by withdrawing the excommunication of four traditionalist bishops who were consecrated illegally, including one who notoriously denies the Holocaust, Ratzinger has confirmed all the fears which arose when he was elected pope. The Pope favours people who still reject the freedom of religion affirmed by Vatican II, dialogue with other churches, reconciliation with Judaism, a high esteem for Islam and the other world religions and the reform of the liturgy.

In order to advance 'reconciliation' with a tiny group of arch-reactionary traditionalists, the Pope risks losing the trust of millions of Catholics all over the world who continue to be loyal to Vatican II. That it is a German Pope who is taking such false steps heightens the conflicts. Apologies after the event cannot put together the pieces.

The Pope would have an easier job than the President of the United States in adopting a change of course. He has no Congress alongside him as a legislative body nor a Supreme Court as a judiciary. He is absolute head of government, legislator and supreme judge in the church. If he wanted to, he could authorise contraception overnight, permit the marriage of priests, make possible the ordination of women and allow eucharistic fellowship with the Protestant churches. What would a Pope do who acted in the spirit of Obama?

Clearly, like Obama he would

1. state clearly that the Catholic Church is in a deep crisis and would identify the heart of the problem: many congregations without priests, still not enough new recruits to the priesthood, and a hidden collapse of pastoral structures as a result of unpopular mergers of parishes, a collapse which has often developed over centuries;

2. proclaim the vision of hope of a renewed church, a revitalised ecumenism, understanding with the Jews, the Muslims and other world religions and a positive assessment of modern science;

3. gather around him the most competent colleagues, not yes-men and women but independent minds, supported by competent and fearless experts;

4. immediately initiate the most important reform measures by decree ('executive order'); and

5. convene an ecumenical council to promote the change of course.

But what a depressing contrast.

Whereas President Obama, with the support of the whole world, is looking forwards and is open to people and to the future, this Pope is orientating himself above all backwards, inspired by the ideal of the medieval church, sceptical about the Reformation, ambiguous about modern rights of freedom.

Whereas President Obama is concerned for new cooperation with partners and allies Pope Benedict XVI, like George W. Bush, is trapped in thinking in terms of friend and foe. He snubs fellow Christians in the Protestant churches by refusing to recognise these communities as churches. The dialogue with Muslims has not got beyond a lip confession of 'dialogue'. Relations with Judaism must be said to have been deeply damaged.

Whereas President Obama radiates hope, promotes civic activities and calls for a new 'era of responsibility', Pope Benedict is imprisoned in his fears and wants to limit human freedom as far as possible, in order to establish an 'age of restoration'.

Whereas President Obama is going on the offensive by using the Constitution and the great tradition of his country as the basis for bold steps in reform, Pope Benedict is interpreting the decrees of the 1962 Reform Council in a backward direction, looking towards the conservative Council of 1870.

But because in all probability Pope Benedict XVI himself will be no Obama, for the immediate future we need:

First, an episcopate which does not conceal the manifest problems of the church but mentions them openly and tackles them energetically at a diocesan level;

Secondly, theologians who collaborate actively in a future vision of our church and are not afraid to speak and write the truth;

Thirdly, pastors who oppose the excessive burdens constantly imposed by the merging of many parishes and who boldly take responsibility as pastors;

Fourthly, in particular women, without whom in many places parishes would collapse, who confidently make use of the possibilities of their influence.

But can we really do this? Yes, we can.

Reproduced with permission from The New York Times Syndicate.

Professor Dr. Hans Kung is a Swiss Catholic priest, controversial theologian, and prolific author. Since 1995 he has been President of the Foundation for a Global Ethic. Kung remains a Catholic priest, but the Vatican has rescinded his authority to teach Catholic theology. Though he had to leave the Catholic faculty, he remained at the University of Tübingen as a professor of Ecumenical Theology, serving as Emeritus Professor since 1996. Neither his bishop nor the Holy See has revoked his priestly faculties.

FATHER PETER KENNEDY:
THE REVOLUTIONARY PRIEST

by Ross Fitzgerald

The sacking of controversial Catholic priest, Peter Kennedy, may have satisfied some conservative forces, but it's not a good look for a church that used to pride itself on its social justice.

Fr Peter Kennedy had hundreds of followers and his church, St Mary's at South Brisbane, was a beacon of enlightened thinking. What business would close down such a successful franchise?

Yet Fr Kennedy's licence to exercise the rights of priestly office has been revoked for his refusal to stop outlawed practices such as allowing women to preach. Kennedy has been banned from conducting services as a Roman Catholic priest anywhere in the world, while his sidekick, Terry Fitzpatrick, has been banned from being active as a priest in the Catholic Archdiocese of Brisbane. Kennedy's followers also face the possibility of excommunication.

Despite this, almost all of Kennedy's flock from St Mary's have followed him to his temporary 'church' at the nearby Brisbane Trades and Labour Council Building. Indeed around 1000 people a week currently attend 'St Mary's-in-Exile' with services held at 6:30 p.m. on Saturday, and 9 a.m. and 5 p.m. on Sunday. In contrast, the official St Mary's, which has now cancelled one of its services, currently attracts less than 100 worshippers a week.

As yet, no attempt has been made to interpret the battle between the institutional Church on the one hand, and Fr Kennedy and his many followers on the other, within a wider Queensland, Australian and global context. This needs to be done because the Catholic Church has been an influential force in Australian society and political life.

Australian Catholics have contributed widely and sometimes controversially to the rich tapestry of our public life. In his seminal history, *The Roman Mould of the Australian Catholic Church*, John Molony traverses the various conflicts within Australian Catholicism, some of them reflective of global tensions, between a rebellious and nationalistic Irish episcopate – led by Melbourne's Archbishop Daniel Mannix – and attempts by Rome to bring them to heel. Yet the replacement of English Benedictines by Irishmen like Mannix signified a concession to the view that the Colonial Office should not run the Australian branch of the Catholic Church, and that no vestige of the subordinate position of restorationist Catholicism of the United Kingdom should taint the Australian Catholic experience.

From time to time, Rome has attempted to bring its rebellious Australian cadres into line through the appointment of disciplinary and interfering bishops and nuncios, but the historical record shows that Australian Catholics subscribe overwhelmingly to the political and cultural values of the secular state, and have remained firmly opposed to an established church.

When, during World War II, Archbishop Giovanni Panico was appointed Apostolic Delegate to Australia, he actively campaigned for the appointment of native-born Australian priests as Bishops and Archbishops, instead of Irish-born priests. This was seen as a very controversial move in some quarters of the Catholic Church in Australia.

So where does Peter Kennedy fit into this distinctly Australian tradition – in which respect for authority has to be measured against the capacity of authority to show leadership, command respect, and engage critically with contemporary culture?

During the authoritarian regime of National Party premier Johannes Bjelke-Petersen, Kennedy was part of the opposition of the Queensland Catholic Church, with the tacit approval of his then Archbishop, Francis Rush, to the moral and political excesses of the corrupt and authoritarian Queensland government. For example, Kennedy invited several key players, including myself (then widely known as an 'Anti-Joh') and Tony Fitzgerald QC (who presided over the Commission of Inquiry into Queensland police and governmental corruption) to address his congregation. This was a clear testament to the engaged nature of his pastorate.

In many areas, Kennedy deliberately brought the Gospels to engage with public life. And what a difference it made to engage with a priest who was well read, articulate and passionately involved with his audience, whether indigenous or white, atheist or believer, Protestant or Catholic, male or female, straight or gay.

Kennedy offered an alternative model of Catholicism, one that is not as unique as is sometimes thought, but which is decreasingly tolerated as global Catholicism becomes more monochromatic and is reining in the so-called 'excesses' of Vatican II reforms. Indeed, far from pleading guilty to excesses, Kennedy and his following convincingly argue that the rolling back of renewal has been on the part of the mainstream Catholic Church and its episcopate.

At a global level, the turning back of the clock began in earnest with the papal election of John Paul II. While the Polish pope was highly successful in helping sound the death knell of communism, his alliance with Ronald Reagan and Margaret Thatcher led him to make toxic compromises with neoconservatives. This conservatism was reflected in a rejection of women as participants and priests in the Church, a matter now firmly closed since John Paul II's papacy. Another issue was John Paul II's crushing of liberation theology, which was the most interesting and relevant flowering of Catholic social teaching since Vatican II. He allowed his anti-communism to override and obliterate new theological and practical approaches to social justice.

Then the Vatican promoted clerics who in many instances were known to have blood on their hands – not simply indirectly through their compliance with policies intended to support corrupt military dictatorships but also through their silence over the murder of hundreds of priests, nuns, bishops and lay people in developing countries. Under the former and current pope, Catholic social teaching has been removed from its pivotal role in Australian Catholic consciousness and identity and replaced by an unhealthy return to Latinist practices that were not so long ago the precise reasons for Vatican II being called.

Father Kennedy's helpmate at St Mary's (and now at St Mary's-in-Exile), Terry Fitzpatrick, is a priest of the Toowoomba Diocese and insofar as he is still a Catholic priest he is simply on leave of absence from the Toowoomba Diocese and has been so for 15 years. This is since he disclosed that he was the father of a boy, Jordan McGuire.

Edward Kelly, then Bishop of Toowoomba, immediately relieved Fitzpatrick of his position and forced him into taking leave of absence. In contrast, the current Bishop, William Morris, took the view that Fitzpatrick had some responsibility for the upbringing of his child and has continued to support him during his extended leave of absence. Jordan, who has taken his mother's surname, has been cared for lovingly by both of his parents.

Unsurprisingly, while Fr Fitzpatrick is not the first priest to father a child – but one of the few to acknowledge it – he has never been officially invited back to Toowoomba, in part because such a move would be deeply opposed by conservative Catholics and other fundamentalists.

Recognising the failures of the Catholic Church to renew itself is essential to an understanding of current events in Brisbane and elsewhere. It is well known that the power given by Vatican II to a commission to change the direction of Church teaching on contraception was revoked at the last minute by curial conservatives concerned as much about their loss of power as their opposition to such practices.

Pope Benedict has further consolidated conservative directions by adverse references to Islam at the time of the Crusades, to Buddhism as a form of autoeroticism, and by proposing that condoms not be used in the fight against AIDS.

In short, at exactly the same time as global consciousness has awoken to the dangers of Islamic fundamentalism, institutional Catholicism, fuelled by a resurgence of fundamentalism in its own ranks, now places increasing obstacles in the path of international peace and justice, and of goodwill to all who inhabit the earth.

To see a once great and well-respected Church, founded on the principle that faith and reason jointly inform a Catholic conscience and sentiment, move in this direction is therefore a profound tragedy. Fr Kennedy is the victim of an institutionalised Church more concerned with papering over the cracks than in cleaning up its own act as a force for good in the world.

Indeed, Kennedy appears to have been made the scapegoat for advocating a socially liberal – and personally inclusive – Catholicism, which is currently so out of favour with Rome.

This article first appeared in shortened form in **New Matilda,** *28 July 2009.*

Emeritus Professor of History and Politics at Griffith, Ross Fitzgerald is a regular columnist for The Weekend Australian *and for* Spectator Australia. *Professor Fitzgerald is the author of 31 books, most recently* The Pope's Battalions: B.A. Santamaria and the Labor Split, *and the co-authored* Under the Influence: a history of alcohol in Australia.

The revolutionary priest in Ross Fitzgerald's prize-winning 1994 novel SOARING (published by Angus & Robertson) is loosely based on Peter Kennedy.

FROM LANDLORD TO EXILE
IN ONE EASY LESSON

by Justin Coleman

I should begin with a disclaimer. For two years, Frs Terry Fitzpatrick and Peter Kennedy used to pay me money. Quite a bit of it, and regularly. When they gave over the St Mary's presbytery to Micah Homelessness Services, they themselves became homeless, which is where I generously stepped up to the mark . . . for a fee.

While I pursued a career in indigenous health in the middle of Nowhere, NT, I became remote landlord to two priests. Decades of training in Catholic guilt meant I felt obliged to return a small percentage to the Sunday plate, but I couldn't complain. As tenants, they were well behaved and generally quiet, particularly as Peter had not yet started his now-YouTube-famous singing lessons.

Twenty-five years ago, my wife's family first drove across town to attend St Mary's and were so impressed by Fr Kennedy, who apparently back then was hirsute and even dashing, that they stayed on. The parish register could annotate my in-laws' family time line with its record of baptisms, weddings and funerals.

When I married into the family and moved to Brisbane, a St Mary's subscription was included as the package deal. Although I 'switched plans' from my parish in Collingwood, which had a similar emphasis on social justice, it certainly wasn't a downgrade. What kept me turning up was the likelihood that, each week, I might learn something about human flourishing, an unravelling of the quintessential question posed by Plato (and doubtless quite a few others since): How best should one live?

Sunday roast–sized servings of sage reflection were dished out at the homily, often by Peter Kennedy or Terry Fitzpatrick, but

112

also by an eclectic mix of various community members who were knowledgeable about various subjects. Plato would have been proud of the philosophical, moral and social breadth of discussion at South Brisbane's meeting place. Unlike in Ancient Greece, women accounted for half the speakers at the forum, a fact which was specifically criticised by the hierarchy in its condemnation of the parish. Women giving sermons . . . who knows what that might lead to next? Communion for homosexuals?

And, if the main meal was always meaty, the proof was in the pudding. Each week, the pews brimmed with parishioners, with every age bracket strongly represented. In Australian churches, the younger demographic is conspicuous by its absence; a 2006 Australian Catholic University report suggests just seven per cent of Catholics aged 20 to 40 years attend Mass. The only churches making inroads seem to be fundamentalist Christian. Yet, here was St Mary's pulling the crowds without any suggestion of offering the somewhat simplistic salvation of the evangelicals.

I have had a lifetime of rewarding involvement with countless inspiring priests, nuns, brothers and Catholic laity. Sadly, however, I have reached a point where – until recently unthinkably – I will not describe myself as 'Catholic' on the next census. The date I came to this decision was 21 February 2009, when Fr Peter Kennedy got his marching orders. I marched with him.

Tellingly, the response of most of my family and Catholic childhood friends will not be 'Why?' but 'What took you so long?' or its variation, 'Who cares?' This response from a family of wonderfully Catholic symmetry – my paternal grandparents had five children, each of whom had five children – and where, dangling from every second branch of the genealogical tree on both sides is a Jesuit, Christian Brother or Catholic school teacher. One grandfather spent half his life fundraising for Newman College at Melbourne University, while my other grandfather had our local Kew parish garden named after him: he nurtured the rose beds as the church nurtured him. Today, his rose bushes have all withered and died; I could construct a brilliant metaphorical causation, but the Victorian drought probably had a hand in it, too.

In many ways, my leaving the Church marks me as typical of my generation; the overwhelming majority of us now in our thirties and forties have, in practice, left the institution, even if many would still put the C word on the census form. Few of our children will grow up with an active interest in the mainstream churches, even though many will attend Catholic schools. My lapsed peers can't believe that the greatest wrath of the institution is reserved for the bloke who actually still turns up to Mass. I'd have more chance of getting a Brisbane Archdiocese job as an atheist than as someone who attends St Mary's-in-Exile.

Ironically, although we have always attended Mass fairly regularly, I have never taken a pew so often – one could say religiously – since it became clear our beloved parish was under threat. The eternal struggle to pile five of us into the car meant I had never needed to learn the first verses of any opening hymn – until a year ago, when the battle with the church hierarchy stirred my slumberous fires of congregational duty.

Arriving early even allowed me to join the music ensemble: I have the Vatican police to thank for dusting the cobwebs off my guitar. I joined an incredibly dedicated bunch of church musos. St Mary's would rival Hillsong if only they could convince the congregation to clap hands.

Although the reflective emphasis on social justice and living for others was what kept me coming back for another helping, the services certainly never lacked Catholic prayer and ritual. Personally, I could have done with a little less of it, particularly given my newfound punctuality, as the payoff would have been shorter Masses. But this would contrast with most of my fellow parishioners, for whom the Catholic 'feel' was crucial.

Ironic, then, that the allegation against the parish was that it was 'out of communion with the Catholic church'. If a thousand Catholics from all walks of life turn up each week to say Catholic prayers, sing Catholic songs and participate in an obviously Catholic ritual led by Catholic priests, it seems ingenuous to override this evidence with that of incorrect vestments (guilty as charged) and lack of emphasis on Trinitarian theology (in hot dispute).

The gradually introduced changes at St Mary's posed no calamitous threat to the wider Brisbane diocese. We never evangelistically sought converts to the one, holy South Brisbane church! There was no explicit expectation that other parishes must follow in our enlightened wake. Before its capitalisation, the word catholic meant broad-minded, and our parish merely offered one type of worship for those so inclined. If the words, garments and ritual of the traditional mass were tinkered with over the years, it was not to promote revolution, but rather evolution.

Like it or not, evolution is essential if any organism is to survive in a changing environment, even a creature as weighty and seemingly anchored as the Catholic Church. Over two millennia, the Church has continually evolved: the only variables being the rate and direction of change. Some of our idiosyncratic ideas at St Mary's will inevitably peter out. Others might be recognised as sensible, good ideas and eventually become mainstream. We weren't the first to use gender-inclusive language and I would be surprised if one day future Catholics don't look back on the all-male vernacular of traditional prayers as curious museum pieces.

The snag was that the Archbishop never actually turned up to find out if the allegations about lack of proper reverence were valid. He set foot in St Mary's once in its last fifteen years, so presumably was relying on either hearsay or surreptitious audio and video recordings taken as things were turning nasty. How easy for the interlopers to distil an hour's prayerful mass to a minute or two of irregular Eucharistic prayer before passing it on as evidence. In an ABC interview in February 2009, the Archbishop explained that, although he had received invitations to attend St Mary's, he didn't get time to visit all the parishes within his Archdiocese. Comforting to know we weren't singled out, then.

The orchestrations of Peter Kennedy's removal turned into a media frenzy, despite the best efforts of the Church to remove him quietly. The Archbishop wrote 'at no stage did I ever want the present drama to be played out in the media', yet the Church-controlled press didn't seem to hold back, running only those stories supporting the official Church's stance and refusing to publish letters with a contrary opinion. The Archdiocese media releases ensured their offer of former High Court judge Ian Callinan as a 'mediator' hit the headlines, even if, as it turned out, the only mediation allowed would be whether Fr Kennedy should leave the keys to the parish house in the letterbox or under the pot plant.

But St Mary's was a story which was never going to die quietly. Its elevation to national news was rapid and sustained, attracting attention from the loony fringes (the Raelians appeared at the church on the last day) to the conservative right (Tess Livingstone, Cardinal Pell's biographer, wrote regular condemnatory articles in *The Australian*). A statue of a Buddhist monk, which few parishioners even knew existed, had its Venus de Milo moment in the spotlight when it was smashed.

The media could smell an enticing story a mile off: a priest falling from grace who, refreshingly, was at no stage accused of anything immoral. Media is a numbers game and, whilst the 15 per cent of Catholics who still attend Mass had divided opinions, the interest from the other 85 per cent was palpable. I suspect for many of those, the whole shebang summed up why the Church had become irrelevant to them. The fact that a naturally introverted man nearing retirement became a media darling was as much due to the David and Goliath nature of the story, as to Peter Kennedy himself. That said, he did fast develop a keen eye for the TV camera, even if not the dress sense.

One factor fanning the flames was that both key protagonists, the Archbishop and his subordinate, had 'a bit of the Irish in them' when it came to a fight. Whilst I doubt either would have considered boxing as a career (and Kennedy, at least, wouldn't even tip the scales into featherweight without some serious binge eating), nor would either back away from taking a stance when they felt they were in the right. And in this stoush, both undoubtedly felt it was worth digging the heels in, for the greater good.

A second factor was the calibre of those who attended the parish. Although it was a mixed bag, often featuring an inebriated resident or two from the St Vincent de Paul hostel next door, its congregation and supporters included noted writers, lawyers, ex-religious and journalists (possibly including a couple from next door). Even a hack guitarist or two. St Mary's attracted more Catholic independent school principals, deputies and religion coordinators than any other parish in Brisbane, although most, understandably, kept their heads down as the publicity gained momentum. When my son's secondary school teacher asked how many students in the class of 25 regularly attended Mass, only three raised their hands. All three attended South Brisbane.

I confess, in hoping that the influence of the congregation might save St Mary's, I had naively underestimated the willingness of the church to cop public flak and weather criticism. I had assumed that an institution already battered by two disinterested generations would be reluctant to lose two of its priests and one of its most thriving parishes. After all, the priest shortage is so critical that even Cardinal Pell has described Australia as the hardest nation in the world in which to gain vocations. Indeed, Archbishop Bathersby delayed his final decision on St Mary's over summer because of travel commitments to Nigeria to seek new priests for Australia's understaffed parishes.

However, I have since realised that the confrontation at St Mary's was merely a blip on the Roman radar. Presumably the loss of a thousand parishioners (minus the two or three who stayed on to attend St Mary's under the new priest) was seen as unfortunate but necessary collateral damage. The Church will outlive any cries of protest.

Meanwhile, as regards the current Catholic Church leaders, to borrow an inappropriately democratic phrase: you've lost my vote. I'm sure you won't lose too much sleep in the Vatican over my decision, but allow me to add a proviso. I hereby declare; if your future leaders follow the advice of John XXIII to 'open the windows of the Church to let in some fresh air'; if that breeze clears out the current Vatican incumbents whose prime concern is orthodoxy (right beliefs), rather than orthopraxis (right practice); and if the new leaders—maybe even some of them female—believe in accountability to the laity; then I promise to rejoin the flock and even tick 'Catholic' on the next census form.

Tempting? If you're interested, let my people talk to your people. Meanwhile, you'll find me strumming away in the TLC building in South Brisbane on a Sunday morning.

Dr Justin Coleman is a General Practitioner originally from Melbourne, who has worked mostly in rural and remote areas. He currently practises at Inala Indigenous Health Service, Brisbane. He has been a columnist in two Victorian newspapers, published hundreds of articles in the medical and general media, edited four medical texts and has published a stage play. He alternates between academic writing and fiction, only occasionally confusing the two.

SHATTER

by Brian Doyle

The most extraordinary moment of my Catholic lifetime was when little Angelo Roncalli politely grabbed the Church he loved by its ancient hoary arrogant throat and shook it until the dust fell like snow.

But that was nearly fifty years ago, and that twenty-third John died before he could bend the biggest corporation on earth back toward its original incredible idea, relentless love, and away from its addiction to control, and since then the hierarchy, up to and including the remarkable man who now steers the ship, has maybe been more interested in conserving power than in correcting pride.

The priesthood, including the late public relations genius of the last pope, has in general wished to protect the cherished idea of a paternal and pastoral Church that led and taught its flock, even as the flock increasingly found many of the men who vow to be their servants uninterested in and dismissive of what they thought and how they lived.

Which is why in my lifetime millions of American Catholics, including me, have saluted the hierarchy with respect and often affection even as they steeled their resolve to make their own moral decisions.

And then came revelations of rape, and more rapes, rapes beyond counting, more rapes than we will ever know, and is there a more horrible and evil phrase than that? But none of us, not even cowards like the bishops and cardinals who with their lies let children be raped and ruined in their parishes, knew the true horror – how many twisted troubled priests there were and are, how many cruel inept bishops, how deep the squirming evil in the corporation expressly designed to fight evil. 'The smoke of Satan', as the American bishops themselves have said. I have three small children; I am enraged; I am afraid; I am bitter. The organisation into which I was born, in which I was schooled, to which I have devoted much of my professional life, was caught with its pants down, revealed to be a place where men at the highest levels shut their eyes to the screams of children in the next room.

Yet this acid bath may heal the church, may force it back into the clean future little Angelo Roncalli dreamed for it; and so might, I venture to guess, events like the recent turmoil at St Mary's in Brisbane, and the irrepressible, unquenchable voices of wild Catholic writers like the late Andre Dubus, and the growing quiet insistence of Catholic universities worldwide that they have a primary role in the Catholic story in the 21st century, and the stunning transfer of ownership of many parishes from diocese to congregation. From these sea changes may come a new Church – one that will, I pray quietly, be what it has always had the extraordinary potential to be: a stunning voice against poverty and hunger and greed and violence, a force beyond national and political and ethnic snarling, a clan of brothers and sisters bound by the insane faith that love will conquer blood.

A clan, an idea, a force, an energy, a prayerful verb that reaches for its brothers and sisters among other faiths and creeds; that reunites with other Christian faiths and with its parent and root, Judaism; that links arms with the other faiths that sense the One under all; that joins hands with the faiths that chase the holy miracle of life and call it many names; and together, the motley clan now comprising most of the people in the world, dream a new planet.

Probable? No. I am no fool.

Possible? Yes. I believe.

The Catholic hierarchy isn't the Catholic Church. The men and women who take vows as priests and nuns, and the ones who are elevated to authority, like the many dozens of admirable cardinals and bishops in America and around the wild green bruised planet, are overwhelmingly brave and graceful and honest and unbelievably selfless – but they are a tiny percentage of the Catholic world.

So 'the Church' will not be shattered by the horrific unveiling of rape and twisted sex and cowardly mismanagement, or by the power struggle in Brisbane, or by the Vatican's concerted effort to tell Catholic colleges what to teach, because the Church is us – mothers, fathers, children, single people, gay and divorced and separated men and women, all the people in the fifteenth pew and very many who never sit in pews at all but savour Christ's words in their hearts: the people Father Peter Kennedy opened his church to, the people he insisted were welcome no matter what their status in the corporate body of the formal religion.

What will shatter, what I pray will shatter, is a culture of paranoid power in the Catholic Church – a culture the Church has wrestled with for many centuries, because the Church is a human construct draped on an incredible idea, and human constructs, as you and I know all too well, are utterly liable to violence and greed, craven cupidity, arrogance, lies.

I do not forget the early Church, that band of brothers and sisters who grew up around the ludicrous idea that a young skinny intense devout poetic confusing dazzling Jew preaching love love love was Himself the distilled essence of the unimaginable Force that created all that is. A crazy idea, and they were crazy men and women, addicted to His stunning idea that love would conquer blood.

But they persisted – against the enmity of their Jewish brethren, against the enmity of the world's greatest empire then, against the enmity of time. They did so in the early years by communal love: they chose their own priests from among themselves, they did not fetishise celibacy, they elected their own bishops, they met in fields and forests, they steered clear as best they could from power and money, and tried to stay focused on the young Jew's message, and the carrying of that love to the ends of the earth, the forging of that wild message into a wild new peace, a new way of being, a revolution of the heart.

Inevitably it took an organisation to carry that message, and no organisation can persist for two thousand years without being subject to all the million sins and vices of the human engine: lust, greed, violence. And the Catholic Church has suffered them all in spades, being nothing more and nothing less, ultimately, than a corporation to house and protect the original crazy idea.

The corporation is brave and extraordinary and flawed and cruel. It has been responsible, perhaps, for more blood and death than any other corporation in the history of the world. It is, in its modern incarnation, egregiously mismanaged. It has far too few managers for its workforce – remember, this is a clan and corporation numbering more than a billion people – and those managers are all male, all unmarried, and almost all elderly. It is, despite its worldwide scope and influence, headquartered in a single vast ancient Italian castle where a cadre of mostly Italian men persist in trying to control the lives and loves of people around the planet. It is, despite its own very public cry for openness – *aggiornamento!* – nearly fifty years ago, in real ways closed to women, closed to gay people, closed to divorced people, closed to the very same scattered democracy of the first days after Christ, when a handful of men and women dispersed from Jerusalem to carry the news of a love that did not die.

But I suggest that this closed corporation, which I have loved and hated, which enrages me and has immensely enlivened and enlightened my life, which has fueled a million memoirs and movies, which has harboured the most amazing grace and genius and the most savage rape and sin, is dying and being reborn before our eyes. It is crumbling and shattering and turning to ash and roiling and churning and something in its hammered and flinty heart is struggling to be born anew.

I suggest that these days are the first blinking mewling days of the new Church.

I suggest that Peter Kennedy, right and wrong, is the vanguard of a new kind of priest.

I suggest that the Vatican as imperial corporate headquarters may someday become Buckingham Palace, a beloved and respected and necessary and nutritious element of Catholicism, but not at all crucial, and certainly not in charge.

I suggest that the pope will someday be elected not by cardinals but by worldwide acclamation of his people every bit as inspired by the Holy Spirit as their cardinals locked in a room together have been in the past.

I suggest that the Curia will someday be vastly expanded and vastly diluted.

I suggest that synods of bishops around the world will someday really be the leaders of the faithful in their nations, beholden not to Rome but to the people they have sworn to serve.

I suggest that dioceses and archdioceses may someday again elect their own priests and bishops.

I suggest that women will someday take their rightful place in the first rank of teachers and pastors in the church.

I suggest that the financial status of churches and schools and parishes and dioceses and archdioceses, already teetering, will change utterly into entities designed not as outposts of the diocese but as independent spiritual villages in large part devoted once again to what built the American Catholic Church in the 19th and 20th centuries, schools.

I suggest that my church will soon welcome and celebrate its gay members with all its heart, not in the current way of public speech and private disdain.

I suggest that my church will welcome and celebrate its divorced and remarried members without the clownish and Byzantine apparatus of annulment.

I suggest that the legacy of John Paul II will eventually be not his continued marginalisation of women and insistence on corporate control, but his ferocious insistence that Christ's message can destroy totalitarian governments without smart bombs, that wars are inarguably failures of the imagination, and that we are brothers and sisters with all people who pursue holiness.

I suggest that my church will slowly but eventually turn itself over, as it were; that its leaders in the future will be lay men and women, and the hierarchy, a brave and creative and committed and admirable tiny minority, will be celebrated for the extraordinary choice of life they have made, not feared for the crimes they may commit.

I suggest that my church will always be a struggle and a mess, will always be a human yearning and failure, will always be striving and falling, will always be a house for wonder and woe, will never be what it wishes to be; but will be closer to the spirit of its astounding and miraculous birth, in the years to come, than it has been in two millennia. And that, my friends, is a miracle.

The Catholic idea, all these years after Christ died and rose and his friends scattered around the world on their incredible public relations mission, remains stunning and unbelievable – and crucial.

And the church which eventually enfleshed that idea, the church which has meant so much to so many, which has meant so much to Western civilisation, which has in the most real sense imaginable saved so many souls and so many lives from despair, stands now at a crossroads the like of which it has not faced since the Emperor Constantine saw a sword of fire in the sky and reconsidered the whole idea of massacre of Christians. It will, in the years to come, fall into dusty insignificance, or be reborn and resurrected in a wild motley creative roiling singing form we can only dimly see; but I hope and pray with all my heart that before I die I see clear a church that matters more than it has since the skinny dusty confusing mysterious gaunt testy riveting devout Jew Yesuah ben Joseph selected his first team and so birthed an idea that might heal the bruised and wondrous world.

Amen and then again amen.

Brian Doyle is the editor of Portland Magazine *at the University of Portland, in Oregon, USA. He is the author of nine books, most recently* Thirsty for the Joy: Australian & American Voices.

KEEPING FAITH IN DIFFICULT TIMES

by Veronica Brady

I am old enough to have experienced the glory days of the 1960s when the visionary Pope John XXIII called the Second Vatican Council to bring about an *aggiornamento* (a renewal of life) in a Church which had grown increasingly out of touch with the world in which we lived. After teaching in High School for some years I found myself in Canada at the University of Toronto, studying for a doctorate there. That in itself was liberating, of course, since I had moved out of the relatively narrow world of a Catholic school and convent life, more or less set apart from the rest of the world, into the wider community – in my case into the life of a graduate student, sharing ideas and experiences and making friends with my fellow students.

It was a lively time. The Vietnam War was drawing to its end and anti-war protests and marches were increasing – several of my fellow students, for example, were young Americans who had fled to Canada to escape the draft – and the Civil Rights Movement was at its height. Looking back, I suppose, I felt then rather like the poet Wordsworth in the early days of the French Revolution for whom it was 'bliss to be alive' and 'to be young was very heaven'. New possibilities were opening out before me, possibilities I thought I had given up when I entered the convent. But more importantly perhaps, the gap which had grown up between the life I had been living after school – I did not become a nun straight from school but went to university and then taught for a year or so – and my life as a nun was narrowing, especially as far as my understanding of the world was concerned.

But the theological nourishment and inspiration the Council was providing was perhaps even more crucial: as someone has said, its effect on many Catholics at the time was like the trumpets of Joshua's army which brought down the walls of Jericho, opening out the closed and defensive milieu of the Church to the world of our day, reminding us that we were not supposed to be set apart in some special religious enclosure but called to share in the 'hopes and fears, joys and sufferings' of people throughout the world. This has been my central conviction since then. But why am I beginning my reflection on the story of Peter Kennedy in this way? It is, I think, because as I see it his story is linked to the hopes raised by the vision of Church and ministry sparked off by Vatican II on the one hand, but also on the other to what is to me the sad fact of the other by the apparent retreat from them by the institutional Church and its return to an older and narrower model – in this country at least. In that sense, I believe, the story of St Mary's is part of a much larger theological but also socially and historically significant story and one that matters, I believe, for many of us who are trying to preserve our faith in the Catholic Church in this country.

To begin with, however, I should point out that since I live on the other side of the continent I have not been intimately involved in the story and have only heard reports from afar, so that what I will be saying may be inaccurate and merely speculative. At the same time I have found that first impressions are often very accurate and since my impressions of the parish and of what was happening there were of this kind, I may have a contribution to make.

As I recall, I was first invited to St Mary's to speak at a dinner to raise funds for the social works which were an essential part of the life of the parish. This in itself suggested the model of parish which had been in vogue when I was in Toronto, sparked off by Vatican II and was much discussed in the university's Catholic Faculty of Theology where seminarians were being trained for the priesthood. It was a model based on a series of concentric circles with the table of the Eucharist at its centre, then the actual congregation in a particular church, then the local community in which the church was situated, then the inhabitants of the city, then of the nation, of the world as a whole and finally of the cosmos – all caught up in this great act of praise and thanksgiving.

St Mary's was not situated in a prosperous suburb, the area around the church was relatively poor. But most of the parishioners were middle-class professional people, who came from elsewhere. The building across the yard from the church, however, seemed very important for the local community, many of whom were unemployed or supporting mothers or Aboriginal people, some of whom who seemed to like sitting around the church. The building itself was the centre of the parish's outreach, providing advice and assistance to people who came looking for shelter or advice or for food or clothing. All of this was largely supported by the St Mary's congregation, though some money also came from government sources. Evidently the Gospel proclaimed and celebrated in the church across the yard was being lived out here and the congregations at the Sunday Masses also played their part in this work.

At the same time, at Mass gathered around the altar – there were no serried ranks of pews: the church was one large open space – they seemed absorbed in the sacred action, especially, one sensed, at the moment of consecration, when I overheard some repeating softly to themselves the priest's words. While he responded to the Scripture readings, the readers usually offered their own reflections, which were often quite sophisticated theologically. Members of the congregation were also responsible for the Bidding Prayers. This involvement, however, seems to have become the crucial point of tension between Kennedy and the Church authorities, in effect challenging the hierarchical model of Church by giving more responsibility to the laity and thus implicitly emphasising the priesthood of all believers—something the Second Vatican Council had done also.

So what are the rights and wrongs involved here? I am only an amateur theologian. But I believe profoundly in the need for us as Christians to share what we have been given with a world profoundly in need of the Good News. This takes me back to where I began, to my responses so long ago – and indeed the responses of many Catholics – to Vatican II, the excitement of feeling at last that there was a living connection between being Catholic and being a contemporary human being and no longer someone who belonged in some strange elsewhere; and I still remember the shock of answering the phone some years before the Council in the community in which I was living in Sydney, saying (as we did in those days) not 'hello' but 'Loreto convent' and the voice at the other end saying 'Sorry, wrong century' rather than 'Wrong number'.

The kind of community Peter Kennedy was creating at St Mary's was very much part of our present world located in the city of Brisbane in an ordinary and not particularly privileged district. More importantly the priest here did not lord it over his congregation – as some clergy seem to do – or set himself apart in a position of privilege as if he were a special and superior kind of human being. His privilege, it seemed, was to celebrate the Eucharist for and with the community, to administer the sacraments to and for them, to baptise, celebrate the rite of reconciliation and their marriages, bless their dying and their burial, and generally listen to them and be at their service. No doubt he made mistakes and at times was less than perfect. But it is hard to see why there was such tension between him and the Church authorities.

Essentially, as I see it, he seemed to be trying to build the kind of parish envisaged by Vatican II which is based on the model of Jesus himself, at the service of the world in which we live and proclaiming the Good News of love, justice and peace. As a distant onlooker, of course, I do not know the reason or reasons for his dismissal, or even whether perhaps he himself resigned from the priesthood. What troubles me is rather that in the official Catholic Church today in general and in Australia in particular, the Roman model still seems to prevail, a bureaucratic model originally based on that of the Roman Empire, in which, as Paul might say, the Law seems more powerful than the Spirit and prophets are regarded with suspicion and the defence of the status quo as the crucial task.

It troubles me as someone inspired so long ago by the Council's vision of Church in tune with and at the service of the 'joys and pains, hopes and fears' of men and women of our time with the power to transform them and help us heal the wounds of our suffering world; it is deeply disappointing that the official Church seems to have been unable to tolerate the existence of a community like St Mary's. The theology underpinning this position seems implicitly based on the idea of a remote and authoritarian God with little feeling for or understanding of the world we live in who seems the 'God of the Philosophers' (as Pascal called him) rather that the God who came among us in Jesus of Nazareth and whose Spirit – to borrow an image from the great theologian Karl Barth – flows through this world like a river. As Barth also goes on to warn us, however, rivers have a habit of changing course, so that it is possible that some of us may be sitting on the banks of a watercourse which has dried up since the river has flowed elsewhere. To be a Christian, as Scripture reminds us, is to be a pilgrim, perpetually on our way to realise the dreams of God for us which are much larger and richer than any we could construct for ourselves.

Veronica Brady is a Catholic nun, member of the Institute of The Blessed Virgin Mary (the Loreto Sisters), who has taught in the English Department of the University of Western Australia where since her retirement she is now an Honorary Senior Research Fellow. She has a longstanding interest in Australian literature, culture and belief and has published widely in the area. Her most recent books are South of My Days, *a biography of Judith Wright, and* The God-shaped Hole, *a collection of essays.*

MARY, MARY QUITE CONTRARY –
FR KENNEDY, ST MARY'S AND VATICAN II

by Neil Ormerod

It is now over 40 years since the conclusion of the Second Vatican Council. Those of us who lived through its years can attest to the immediate impact it had on our lives. Changes in liturgical and sacramental practice spread through the church like wildfire. For some it was liberating, for some aggravating and for all disorienting. We would often hear appeals to the 'spirit of the Council' as justification for the wide variety of changes we faced. Few who lived though that period would doubt the epochal significance of the Council.

Yet increasingly the significance of the changes produced by the Council has been subject to debate. On the one side there is the Bologna school of Church history which some claim emphasises the 'rupture' of the council. On the other side is a more official interpretation which so emphasises the continuity as to rule out any possibility of discontinuity. John Paul II stated in 2000 that 'to read the council as if it marked a break with the past . . . is decidedly unacceptable'.

It is not difficult to see these divergent positions in operation in the Australian Church. We need only witness the recent events in the St Mary's parish in South Brisbane. While Archbishop John Bathersby called upon the parish to return to full communion with the archdiocese, the people of the parish proclaim that it is a 'Vatican II parish' and that they 'love Vatican II', implying that somehow the Archbishop does not support the changes the Council sought to implement.

At the core of that conflict we can identify divergent understandings of the significance of the Council and the changes, and the limits of those changes, it introduced into Church life. Indeed it is very difficult to conceive of such a conflict arising prior to the event of the Council. The solidity of the pre–Vatican II Church bordered on complete immobility. Change when it was introduced by the Council was rapid and generally poorly handled by Church authorities, with little explanation or rationale. And many of the changes which occurred went beyond those envisaged by the Council. Any reading of the document on the liturgy, for example, makes it clear that the Council Fathers expected Latin to continue as a liturgical language, yet in quick time it was completely replaced by the vernacular. The process of rapid change created an expectation of further change in a whole range of issues – birth control, ecumenical and interfaith dialogue, women in ministry and so on. The questions which emerged from this period are: Are there limits to such change? If so what are they? And who determines them? Much energy from the Vatican since the Council has been expended in clarifying the boundaries of change, on what is acceptable and what is beyond the pale.

To take a concrete example, in the course of his conflict with the Archbishop, Fr Peter Kennedy publicly called into question the divinity of Jesus:

'If I'm going to be true to myself, I would rather believe that Jesus was a human person rather than what the Church teaches, that Jesus is a divine person with a human and divine nature. I would tend rather to agree with Arius that Jesus was a human person. Now when I say that, I am quite sure that in your church community across the parish community, you would have so many people with their understanding of Jesus, and it wouldn't be necessarily that strict understanding of the hierarchy. But see, once you start to question, once you even start to question, even to dialogue, that's all I'd like to do; like, I'm quite open to being convinced that Jesus was a divine person.'

While one might quibble over the theological and historical accuracy of Fr Kennedy's account of Arius, the more recent lineage of the position he articulates is the work of Piet Schoonenberg, a Dutch theologian writing not long after the Council. More recently it has been popularised by Australian author Michael Morwood. At stake is not so much the debate between Arius and the bishops of the Council of Nicea, but the later Council of Chalcedon which defined belief in the one person and two natures of Christ. The position that Jesus was a human person with a human nature had been raised by Nestorius, and rejected. It was unclear how such a position was compatible with any sense of Jesus being truly divine. In that regard Fr Kennedy's concession that 'I'm quite open to being convinced that Jesus was a divine person' is hardly a stirring affirmation of what many would consider a central Christian belief.

Such a 'change' in belief is not just something the bishops of Vatican II didn't get around to suggesting, it is something they would have rejected root and branch as a denial of the very meaning of Christianity. Every document of the Council makes clear their unequivocal commitment to traditional Christian Trinitarian and Christological doctrine. And when various authors such as Schoonenberg or Morwood have made similar suggestions about Jesus, Church authorities have not been slow to respond. These central Trinitarian and Christological beliefs have been the common stance not just of the Catholic Church but of Christianity in general and any departure from them must meet a heavy burden of proof. When Fr Kennedy says he is open to being convinced that Jesus is a divine person, one might distinguish between doubt about the fact – whether Jesus was a divine person or not – and doubt about whether this is what Christians believe – whether this is a proper account of Christian belief. Though many might struggle with the precise formulation, there is no doubt in my mind this belief is constitutive of Christian identity.

Fr Kennedy is of course entitled to believe what he likes, but he is not therefore entitled to give it the name 'Catholic' or 'Christian' or to suggest that those who disagree are just being 'conservative' or not operating in the 'spirit of Vatican II'. When he pleads for dialogue one must ask how one would approach such dialogue. Is it with a fellow believer seeking to clarify the terms of belief or with a non-believer seeking to be convinced or converted to that belief? Certainly questions can be raised, but some presumption remains that answers given within the tradition demand a solid hearing. Of course, one might question a happily married man whether he really loves his wife, but one would hardly be surprised if persistent questioning produced a rather heated response. Similarly there is something disingenuous when people are surprised at the response of Church authorities when central Christian beliefs are called into question, particularly by people one would normally think have a responsibility to uphold those beliefs.

Of course, Vatican II said many things, on the role of the laity, on ecumenical and interfaith dialogue, on the importance of returning to the Scriptures as the source of faith and so on. However, it also had important things to say on the role of the Bishop, such as: 'Among the principal duties of bishops the preaching of the Gospel occupies an eminent place. For bishops are preachers of the faith, who lead new disciples to Christ, and they are authentic teachers, that is, teachers endowed with the authority of Christ, who preach to the people committed to them the faith they must believe and put into practice, and by the light of the Holy Spirit illustrate that faith.' (Lumen Gentium n.25)

One might wonder whether those parishioners who wore T-shirts stating that they 'love Vatican II' were aware of this particular statement and 'loved' it as well. It speaks clearly of the authority of the bishop and his responsibility to uphold and teach the Catholic faith. They are called upon to 'preach to the people committed to them the faith they must believe and put into practice.' I can feel nothing but empathy for Archbishop Bathersby, a truly decent and generous person, who found himself caught between a rock and a hard place. In acting to remove Fr Kennedy he will be attacked as a 'conservative' or a puppet of the Vatican; failing to do so he knows he would not be fulfilling his responsibility as a bishop to teach the faithful 'the faith they must believe'. He deserved better than this.

For his part, it seems to me that Fr Kennedy has portrayed himself as the stereotypical 'little Aussie battler' being set upon by harsh and unjust Church authorities, who are locked in the past, unwilling to consider change, not really listening to his concerns and so on. It is a 'type' guaranteed to elicit sympathy in an age which is generally suspicious of all authority, and of Church authority in particular. And of course we all know of examples where Church authorities got it wrong in the past. But as John Henry Newman once opined, just because clocks sometimes go fast or slow or break down, doesn't mean we should do away with them. Christianity is a faith built on an authoritative witness, the witness of the disciples to Jesus Christ risen from the dead. This is a more than human authority; it is a revelation from God. As such some beliefs are simply non-negotiable to Christian identity. Such a recognition is not new and can be found in the foundational documents of the New Testament itself. 'Many deceivers have gone out into the world. Those who do not confess that Jesus Christ has come in the flesh; any such person is the deceiver and the anti-Christ' (2 John 7).

Many of Fr Kennedy's supporters point out that the parish of St Mary's has a strong record in the area of social justice and inclusion. Archbishop Bathersby has commended the parish for this record on more than one occasion. However, it is hard to see why this record can only be maintained with liturgical anomalies and doctrinal errors. Dorothy Day of the Catholic Workers Movement managed to marry strong social activism with a conservative religious life. The two are not mutually exclusive. Other supporters point out that the parish attracts large numbers of parishioners, while other parishes are in decline. But then so does the Pentecostal church at Hillsong; and so did the 'Little Pebble' in Wollongong before he was carted off to prison. Popularity is a fickle guide to anything really. Indeed in an age suspicious of authorities, notoriety is almost guaranteed to produce popularity! In the end the issue is whether or not the parish was still operating as a Catholic parish. The responsibility to decide in this matter lies with the bishop, not with the parish itself or its parish priest, for Catholic identity is not the preserve of any single parish or individual priest. Key issues for such an evaluation will be whether it upholds central Christian and Catholic beliefs and whether it acknowledges the authority of the local bishop. Where these are lacking, one can hardly be surprised by the final outcome.

Neil Ormerod is Professor of Theology at Australian Catholic University and has published widely in Australia and overseas. His book Creation, Grace and Redemption *(Orbis 2007) received a commendation from the US Catholic Press Association. His most recent book is* Globalization and the mission of the Church *with Pentecostal theologian Shane Clifton.*

A MANIFESTO

by John Shelby Spong

I have made a decision. I will no longer debate the issue of homosexuality in the church with anyone. I will no longer engage the biblical ignorance that emanates from so many right-wing Christians about how the Bible condemns homosexuality, as if that point of view still has any credibility. I will no longer discuss with them or listen to them tell me how homosexuality is 'an abomination to God,' about how homosexuality is a 'chosen lifestyle,' or about how through prayer and 'spiritual counseling' homosexual persons can be 'cured.' Those arguments are no longer worthy of my time or energy. I will no longer dignify by listening to the thoughts of those who advocate 'reparative therapy,' as if homosexual persons are somehow broken and need to be repaired. I will no longer talk to those who believe that the unity of the church can or should be achieved by rejecting the presence of, or at least at the expense of, gay and lesbian people. I will no longer take the time to refute the unlearned and undocumentable claims of certain world religious leaders who call homosexuality 'deviant.' I will no longer listen to that pious sentimentality that certain Christian leaders continue to employ, which suggests some version of that strange and overtly dishonest phrase that 'we love the sinner but hate the sin.' That statement is, I have concluded, nothing more than a self-serving lie designed to cover the fact that these people hate homosexual persons and fear homosexuality itself, but somehow know that hatred is incompatible with the Christ they claim to profess, so they adopt this face-saving and absolutely false statement. I will no longer temper my understanding of truth in order to pretend that I have even a tiny smidgen of respect for the appalling negativity that continues to emanate from religious circles where the church has for centuries conveniently perfumed its ongoing prejudices against blacks, Jews, women and homosexual persons with what it assumes is 'high-sounding, pious rhetoric.' The day for that mentality has quite simply come to an end for me. I will personally neither tolerate it nor listen to it any longer. The world has moved on, leaving these elements of the Christian Church that cannot adjust to new knowledge or a new consciousness lost in a sea of their own irrelevance. They no longer talk to anyone but themselves. I will no longer seek to slow down the witness to inclusiveness by pretending that there is some middle ground between prejudice and oppression. There isn't. Justice postponed is justice denied. That can be a resting place no longer for anyone. An old civil rights song proclaimed that the only choice awaiting those who cannot adjust to a new understanding was to 'Roll on over or we'll roll on over you!' Time waits for no one.

I will particularly ignore those members of my own Episcopal Church who seek to break away from this body to form a 'new church,' claiming that this new and bigoted instrument alone now represents the Anglican Communion. Such a new ecclesiastical body is designed to allow these pathetic human beings, who are so deeply locked into a world that no longer exists, to form a community in which they can continue to hate gay people, distort gay people with their hopeless rhetoric and to be part of a religious fellowship in which they can continue to feel justified in their homophobic prejudices for the rest of their tortured lives. Church unity can never be a virtue that is preserved by allowing injustice, oppression and psychological tyranny to go unchallenged.

In my personal life, I will no longer listen to televised debates conducted by 'fair-minded' channels that seek to give 'both sides' of this issue 'equal time.' I am aware that these stations no longer give equal time to the advocates of treating women as if they are the property of men or to the advocates of reinstating either segregation or slavery, despite the fact that when these evil institutions were coming to an end the Bible was still being quoted frequently on each of these subjects. It is time for the media to announce that there are no longer two sides to the issue of full humanity for gay and lesbian people. There is no way that justice for homosexual people can be compromised any longer.

I will no longer act as if the Papal office is to be respected if the present occupant of that office is either not willing or not able to inform and educate himself on public issues on which he dares to speak with embarrassing ineptitude. I will no longer be respectful of the leadership of the Archbishop of Canterbury, who seems to believe that rude behavior, intolerance and even killing prejudice is somehow acceptable, so long as it comes from third-world religious leaders, who more than anything else reveal in themselves the price that colonial oppression has required of the minds and hearts of so many of our world's population. I see no way that ignorance and truth can be placed side by side, nor do I believe that evil is somehow less evil if the Bible is quoted to justify it. I will dismiss as unworthy of any more of my attention the wild, false and uninformed opinions of such would-be religious leaders as Pat Robertson, James Dobson, Jerry Falwell, Jimmy Swaggart, Albert Mohler, and Robert Duncan. My country and my church have both already spent too much time, energy and money trying to accommodate these backward points of view when they are no longer even tolerable.

I make these statements because it is time to move on. The battle is over. The victory has been won. There is no reasonable doubt as to what the final outcome of this struggle will be. Homosexual people will be accepted as equal, full human beings, who have a legitimate claim on every right that both church and society have to offer any of us. Homosexual marriages will become legal, recognized by the state and pronounced holy by the church. 'Don't ask, don't tell' will be dismantled as the policy of our armed forces. We will and we must learn that equality of citizenship is not something that should ever be submitted to a referendum. Equality under and before the law is a solemn promise conveyed to all our citizens in the Constitution itself. Can any of us imagine having a public referendum on whether slavery should continue, whether segregation should be dismantled, whether voting privileges should be offered to women? The time has come for politicians to stop hiding behind unjust laws that they themselves helped to enact, and to abandon that convenient shield of demanding a vote on the rights of full citizenship because they do not understand the difference between a constitutional democracy, which this nation has, and a 'mobocracy,' which this nation rejected when it adopted its constitution. We do not put the civil rights of a minority to the vote of a plebiscite.

I will also no longer act as if I need a majority vote of some ecclesiastical body in order to bless, ordain, recognise and celebrate the lives and gifts of gay and lesbian people in the life of the church. No one should ever again be forced to submit the privilege of citizenship in this nation or membership in the Christian Church to the will of a majority vote.

The battle in both our culture and our church to rid our souls of this dying prejudice is finished. A new consciousness has arisen. A decision has quite clearly been made. Inequality for gay and lesbian people is no longer a debatable issue in either church or state. Therefore, I will from this moment on refuse to dignify the continued public expression of ignorant prejudice by engaging it. I do not tolerate racism or sexism any longer. From this moment on, I will no longer tolerate our culture's various forms of homophobia. I do not care who it is who articulates these attitudes or who tries to make them sound holy with religious jargon.

I have been part of this debate for years, but things do get settled and this issue is now settled for me. I do not debate any longer with members of the 'Flat Earth Society' either. I do not debate with people who think we should treat epilepsy by casting demons out of the epileptic person; I do not waste time engaging those medical opinions that suggest that bleeding the patient might release the infection. I do not converse with people who think that Hurricane Katrina hit New Orleans as punishment for the sin of being the birthplace of Ellen DeGeneres or that the terrorists hit the United Sates on 9/11 because we tolerated homosexual people, abortions, feminism or the American Civil Liberties Union. I am tired of being embarrassed by so much of my church's participation in causes that are quite unworthy of the Christ I serve or the God whose mystery and wonder I appreciate more each day. Indeed I feel the Christian Church should not only apologise, but do public penance for the way we have treated people of color, women, adherents of other religions and those we designated heretics, as well as gay and lesbian people.

Life moves on. As the poet James Russell Lowell once put it more than a century ago: 'New occasions teach new duties, Time makes ancient good uncouth.' I am ready now to claim the victory. I will from now on assume it and live into it. I am unwilling to argue about it or to discuss it as if there are two equally valid, competing positions any longer. The day for that mentality has simply gone forever.

This is my manifesto and my creed. I proclaim it today. I invite others to join me in this public declaration. I believe that such a public outpouring will help cleanse both the church and this nation of its own distorting past. It will restore integrity and honor to both church and state. It will signal that a new day has dawned and we are ready not just to embrace it, but also to rejoice in it and to celebrate it.

Reprinted with permission from WATERFRONTMEDIA, Bishop Spong's on line publisher. Those who wish to correspond with Bishop Spong may go to his WaterfrontMedia website at www.johnshelbyspong.com

John Shelby Spong served the Episcopal Church as a priest and bishop for forty-five years. As a visiting lecturer at Harvard and at universities and churches throughout North America and the English-speaking world, he is one of the leading spokespersons for an open and engaged Christianity. His twenty-plus books, including The Sins of Scripture, A New Christianity for a New World, *and his autobiography* Here I Stand *have sold over one million copies and have been translated into most of the major languages of the world.*

A NEW MODEL OF BEING CHURCH

by Roy Bourgeois

Growing up in a small town in Louisiana, as Catholics, we did not question our segregated schools or ask why the black members of our Church had to sit in the last five pews during Mass. Nor did we, needless to say, question why women could not be priests. Being a good Catholic also meant being patriotic. So, after college, I entered the military and volunteered for duty in Vietnam, believing the cause was noble, as many of our Church leaders said.

Vietnam became that turning point in my life. The violence, death, and madness of the war drove me into the arms of God. And, for the first time in my life, I started questioning the policies of the leaders in my country and my Church. That questioning has not stopped. I discovered that the prophet Isaiah was right when he said, 'They will take evil and call it good. They will take a life and call it truth.'

I left Vietnam grateful to be alive and wanted to become a peacemaker. I entered Maryknoll, was ordained in 1972, and was sent to serve the poor of Bolivia. A slum on the outskirts of La Paz became my home and the poor became my teachers. They taught me about their struggle and oppression under a brutal dictator, General Hugo Banzer, who my country supported and kept in power. In my fifth year I was among the many arrested and was expelled from Bolivia.

Back in the United States, I was assigned to Maryknoll's peace and justice work. In my travels and talks at churches and colleges around the country, I met with a number of women who shared with me their deep faith and their call to priesthood in the Catholic Church.

In the beginning, like most men, I resisted what the women were saying. However, over time I was compelled to ask myself a few questions that every priest and Catholic should ask: If we, as people of faith, profess that God created men and women of equal stature and dignity, if we say that the call to priesthood comes from God, then who are we, as men, to say to women, 'Our call is valid, but yours is not'? Does not the call to priesthood come from God? Who are we as men, to tamper with the sacred? Who are we to negate God's call of women to the priesthood?

I know an injustice when I see one. As a Catholic priest for 36 years, I have come to see clearly that the exclusion of women from the priesthood is a grave injustice against women, and a grave injustice against the God who calls them to be priests. For years I have been speaking out against the injustice of US foreign policy in Latin America. In conscience, I could not remain silent about an injustice in my Church.

Our Church leaders tell us that women cannot be ordained because Jesus chose only men as apostles. Well, this is not accurate. As Christians, we know the importance of the resurrection. It is at the heart of our faith. It was Mary Magdalene to whom Jesus first appeared after his resurrection. It was Mary Magdalene and other women who were chosen by Jesus to bring the 'good news' of his resurrection to Peter and the other male apostles who, out of fear, were hiding behind closed doors.

It is important to note that when Mary Magdalene and other women were chosen by Jesus to bring the important news to the men, the men did not believe the women. Today, 2000 years later, men still do not believe women when they say, 'We are also chosen by Jesus to be leaders in the Church. We are also called by our loving God, who created men and women of equal stature and dignity, to the priesthood.'

Our Church is in crisis! Hundreds of Catholic churches in the United States are closing due to a shortage of priests! When I entered Maryknoll in 1966, our Order had over 300 seminarians studying for the priesthood. Today we have seven. Seminaries around the country are empty. Our all-male priesthood in the Catholic Church is going the way of the dinosaurs.

If we are to have a vibrant and healthy Church we need the faith, wisdom, experience, compassion, and courage of women in the priesthood. The time has arrived in the long history of the Church to break our silence and create a new model of being Church. The poor of Bolivia taught me that change does not come from the top down, but from the bottom up – from the grassroots. We are the grassroots of our Church and we are being called to walk in solidarity, as Jesus would, with the women in our Church who are being called by God to the priesthood.

The Vatican's Congregation for the Doctrine of the Faith has informed me that if I do not recant my belief and public statements that support the ordination of women in our Church then I will be excommunicated. After much reflection, I wrote the Vatican saying that, in conscience, I cannot recant.

In Louisiana I discovered that God does not bless racism. In Vietnam I discovered that God does not bless war. In Bolivia I discovered that God does not bless oppression. And now, in my Church, I have discovered that God does not bless sexism.

Reprinted with kind permission of the author.

Roy Bourgeois is a Maryknoll priest and founder of the School of the Americas Watch Movement. He was ordained a Catholic priest in 1972 and worked with poor of Bolivia for five years. He was arrested in Bolivia and forced to leave the country for his defence of the poor and became an outspoken critic of US foreign policy in Latin America. Since then has spent over four years in US federal prisons for nonviolent protests against the training of Latin American soldiers at Fort Benning, Georgia.

In 1990, founded the School of Americas Watch and was recipient of the 1997 Pax Christi USA Teacher of Peace Award.

In 1995 he produced a documentary film about the School of Americas called School of Assassins *which received an Academy Award nomination. He travels extensively, giving talks at universities, churches and groups around the country about US foreign policy in Latin America and the ordination of women in the Catholic Church.*

TO THE CONGREGATION FOR THE DOCTRINE OF THE FAITH, THE VATICAN

I was very saddened by your letter dated October 21, 2008, giving me 30 days to recant my belief and public statements that support the ordination of women in our Church, or I will be excommunicated.

I have been a Catholic priest for 36 years and have a deep love for my Church and ministry.

When I was a young man in the military, I felt God was calling me to the priesthood. I entered Maryknoll and was ordained in 1972.

Over the years I have met a number of women in our Church who, like me, feel called by God to the priesthood. You, our Church leaders at the Vatican, tell us that women cannot be ordained.

With all due respect, I believe our Catholic Church's teaching on this issue is wrong and does not stand up to scrutiny. A 1976 report by the Pontifical Biblical Commission supports the research of Scripture scholars, canon lawyers and many faithful Catholics who have studied and pondered the Scriptures and have concluded that there is no justification in the Bible for excluding women from the priesthood.

As people of faith, we profess that the invitation to the ministry of priesthood comes from God. We profess that God is the Source of life and created men and women of equal stature and dignity. The current Catholic Church doctrine on the ordination of women implies that our loving and all-powerful God, Creator of heaven and earth, somehow cannot empower a woman to be a priest.

Women in our Church are telling us that God is calling them to the priesthood. Who are we, as men, to say to women, "Our call is valid, but yours is not." Who are we to tamper with God's call?

Sexism, like racism, is a sin. And no matter how hard or how long we may try to justify discrimination, in the end, it is always immoral.

Hundreds of Catholic churches in the U.S. are closing because of a shortage of priests. Yet there are hundreds of committed and prophetic women telling us that God is calling them to serve our Church as priests.

If we are to have a vibrant, healthy Church rooted in the teachings of our Savior, we need the faith, wisdom, experience, compassion and courage of women in the priesthood.

Conscience is very sacred. Conscience gives us a sense of right and wrong and urges us to do the right thing. Conscience is what compelled Franz Jagerstatter, a humble Austrian farmer, husband and father of four young children, to refuse to join Hitler's army, which led to his execution. Conscience is what compelled Rosa Parks to say she could no longer sit in the back of the bus. Conscience is what compels women in our Church to say they cannot be silent and deny their call from God to the priesthood. Conscience is what compelled my dear mother and father, now 95, to always strive to do the right thing as faithful Catholics raising four children. And after much prayer, reflection and discernment, it is my conscience that compels me to do the right thing. I cannot recant my belief and public statements that support the ordination of women in our Church.

Working and struggling for peace and justice are an integral part of our faith. For this reason, I speak out against the war in Iraq. And for the last eighteen years, I have been speaking out against the atrocities and suffering caused by the School of the Americas (SOA). Eight years ago, while in Rome for a conference on peace and justice, I was invited to talk about the SOA on Vatican Radio. During the interview, I stated that I could not address the injustice of the SOA and remain silent about injustice in my Church. I ended the interview by saying, "There will never be justice in the Catholic Church until women can be ordained." I remain committed to this belief today.

Having an all male clergy implies that men are worthy to be Catholic priests, but women are not.

According to USA TODAY (Feb. 28, 2008), in the United States alone, nearly 5,000 Catholic priests have sexually abused more than 12,000 children. Many bishops, aware of the abuse, remained silent. These priests and bishops were not excommunicated. Yet the women in our Church who are called by God and are ordained to serve God's people, and the priests and bishops who support them, are excommunicated.

Silence is the voice of complicity. Therefore, I call upon all Catholics, fellow priests, bishops, Pope Benedict XVI and all Church leaders at the Vatican, to speak out loudly on this grave injustice of excluding women from the priesthood.

Archbishop Oscar Romero of El Salvador was assassinated because of his defense of the oppressed. He said, *"Let those who have a voice, speak out for the voiceless."*

Our loving God has given us a voice. Let us speak clearly and boldly and walk in solidarity, as Jesus would, with the women in our Church who are being called by God to the priesthood.

In Peace and Justice,

Rev. Roy Bourgeois, M.M.

TAKING A STAND FOR ROY BOURGEOIS: THE CHURCH HAS BEEN EXCOMMUNICATING SAINTS FOR CENTURIES NOW

by Joan Chittister

Maryknoll priest Roy Bourgeois is under threat of excommunication for giving a homily at the unauthorised priestly ordination of a woman sponsored by the group Roman Catholic Womenpriests. The question, especially for those who know this priest to be a justice-loving, selfless prophet of peace, is how Fr Roy's 'case' will be handled by the Vatican. No doubt about it: the situation is an important one, both for him and for the church who will judge him.

It is important for Fr Bourgeois because it involves the possible fracturing of the commitment of a lifetime.

A man who has given his life for the Gospel, has been one of the Church's most public witnesses for human rights, has stood for the best in the human condition and modelled the highest standards of the priesthood should certainly not end his life a victim of the conscience that has stirred the conscience of a nation.

Roy is doing what a Christian is supposed to do: speaking for the disenfranchised, pursuing justice, witnessing to the love of God. As a missionary in Bolivia, he alerted us to the torture-teaching practices of the Fort Benning, Georgia–based School of the Americas. A US military training centre designed to instruct others in methods of terrorising Central-American peasants working for human rights and just wages, this US-funded war against humanity kept many a dictator in power.

Roy's public protest began with a handful of people and has grown to well over 15000 demonstrators yearly. Thanks to Roy, the public pressure for a change of US policies at the School of the

Americas has become one of the country's – one of the church's –
proudest moments of the last 20 years.

Clearly, Roy is a priest whose courage and credibility have been
tested by the state to the maximum. He's not marginal to anything,
measured by the best standards of both church and state. He is
completely a priest, completely American.

The whole truth, however, is that this particular story is
embedded in a struggle that is much larger than Roy. It is the story
of how the Church itself will, this time, deal with the birth pangs
of conscience and consciousness that mark any society in the midst
of change. The Church has been in this situation before, and the
responses, to our shame, have not always, in the chastening light
of history, been good ones.

Excommunicated saints dot the history of the Church with far
too much regularity: Mary Ward, whose sin was the founding of
a religious life for women in the 17th century that did not require
cloister; 19th-century Mary MacKillop, whose sin was opening
Catholic centres without the permission of the bishop; the Beguines,
a medieval community of non-cloistered women in Belgium,
whose sin was walking the streets and ministering in homes; Fr
Teilhard de Chardin, whose sin was the acceptance of the theory of
evolution; Fr Tissa Balasuriya, whose sin was to seek new ways to
transmit the doctrine of original sin in an Asian culture. All were
precursors of momentous social change whose concerns were not
only ignored by the church but punished.

When the dust settled, however, nobody remembered who
excommunicated the saints who were pioneering a new church,
but everybody remembered the saints. And everybody came to
believe what the saints had attempted to teach.

Reformers who centuries ago called for discussion of the sale
of relics, the use of the vernacular in the liturgy, the review of a
theology that divided people according to 'higher' and 'lower'
vocations, were also excommunicated. Wars were fought and
people died by the thousands on both sides in the attempt to impose
Catholic orthodoxy. Nations were divided to maintain Catholicism.
Women were burned at the stake on behalf of Catholic doctrine.
And in Germany, for instance, one woman was executed simply for
owning a Bible in German. And all those things were done in the
name of God.

But with what success? The effects are painfully clear to this very day.

Nobody remembers the 'sins' of the reformers. Everybody remembers the sin of a church that refused to listen to their concerns and is still 400 years late repenting it. And the things the reformers argued for are now part and parcel of Catholicism itself.

Do we never learn? In our own time, church by fear and intimidation is clearly on the brink of becoming the norm again.

Whole groups are being excommunicated everywhere: Call to Action, Dignity, parishes that seek more participation in making parish decisions, and the Women's Ordination Conference. Even people who voted for Barack Obama have been told by some priests and bishops that they need to go to confession before they go to Communion. And, of course, Roman Catholic Womenpriests is an excommunicated group as well. Despite the fact that over two-thirds of the US Catholic Church approves of the ordination of women, the discussion goes on being repressed, rebuffed and disregarded.

People respond in different ways to this kind of church: Some say, 'Love it or leave it.' Some say, 'Someone had to do it and we agree with them, so count us in on the excommunication.' Some say, 'How is it that we excommunicate priests who stand for the expansion of women's roles in the Church but we do not excommunicate pedophile priests who abuse children?' And some say nothing in public. But they say a great deal in private, to their friends, to their local priests and most of all to their children, who, as a result, carry within them the vision of another world to come.

Intimidation does its job, at least for a while. Only 33 religious of the 3000 people who signed an early petition to Rome on Roy Bourgeois' behalf, for instance, used the initials of their religious communities on the petition. But many other religious signed and did not. That's a sure sign of their concern that their communities would be punished if their identities were known. But they did sign. They do believe. They are talking. They are taking a stand.

Who is winning? The enforcers or the believers? Well, it depends on what you mean by 'winning.' History is clear: it is one thing to enforce behaviour; it is another thing entirely to attempt to chain the mind or enslave the heart forever.

From where I stand, it seems to me that now may well be a time when the Church should proceed with great tenderness, an open mind, a listening heart and a clear sense that, just as in times past, God's future is on the way.

Reprinted with permission of the author from Sr Joan Chittister's webcolumn for the **National Catholic Reporter:** *'From Where I Stand.'*

Sister Joan Chittister is an author, international speaker and executive director of Benetvision in Erie, PA, USA. In 2007, Sr Joan Chittister received the Hans Kung Award from the Association for the Rights of Catholics in the Church and the Outstanding Leadership Award from the Leadership Conference of Women Religious. She has also received eleven honorary doctorates and numerous awards, including the US Catholic's *award for Furthering the Cause of Women in the Church, the Thomas Merton Award by the Merton Center, the Distinguished Alumni Award from Penn State University, and the Thomas Dooley Award from the alumni association of the University of Notre Dame.*

WHO ON EARTH WAS JESUS?

by David Boulton

I knew virtually nothing of St Mary's-in-Exile before I left England on 2 September 2009 for a book tour of Australia and New Zealand. Some friends in the Australian Sea of Faith network had drawn my attention to Peter Kennedy's work, and British members of Catholics for a Changing Church pointed me to the St Mary's website. But it wasn't till an invitation came out of the blue to deliver the homily at the Saturday and Sunday Masses that I got to know the full St Mary's story. And what a story!

My first reaction on receiving Peter's invitation was "Why me? Does this man know what he is doing? I'm not a Catholic. I have one foot firmly planted in the Religious Society of Friends (the Quakers), the other in the British Humanist Association. I've written a book called *The Trouble with God*, and my latest book concentrates on the human Jesus of history rather than the divine Christ of Faith. And this man Peter Kennedy is inviting me to preach at his church – not once, or twice, but three times?"

But it seemed that someone had sent him *Who on Earth was Jesus?* and he'd read it and still *invited* me anyway! I accepted – and what an adventure it turned out to be!

Exiled or breakaway churches can be bitter places. Not St Mary's! I discovered a warm, friendly, joyous community, inclusive, outgoing, fully focused on social justice and the get-your-hands-dirty task of building the republic of heaven! This is what *doing church* should be like everywhere – but all too rarely is!

The St Mary's community has had to face an agonising conflict of loyalties: obedience to Authority, or obedience to Conscience.

Talk the talk, or walk the walk. 'The sound of empty praise and prayer which drowns the cries of need', or 'How can the Lord be neutral when the privileged fleece the poor?' It has made its choice, and in doing so has discovered what church is really about. It's been tough: but *Through all the tumult and the strife / I hear that music ringing; / It sounds and echoes in my soul; / How can I keep from singing?*

Church history is littered with stories of reformers and revolutionaries who got up the noses of the ecclesiastical authorities and were expelled or worse, only to find themselves reclaimed and praised as the true representatives of the faith! I have no idea what the future holds for St Mary's, but I know that progressive Christianity has one more beacon, one more growing point. So 'how can I keep from singing?'

This is the homily I preached at St Mary's-in-Exile, at the Trades and Labour Council Hall, on September 5th and 6th (once I'd found out what a homily was . . .):

Will the Real Jesus Please Stand Up!

Friends, it's a huge pleasure for me to be with you at the famous, celebrated, divinely discontented St Mary's-in-Exile! My wife and I landed in Brisbane this morning after a long flight from London. We've brought with us greetings and solidarity from fellow rebels and subversives: from the Society of Friends, the Quakers (who this summer became the first church in Britain to come out officially in favour of same-sex marriage); from the Sea of Faith Network, which puts its faith in questions rather than answers; and from Catholics for a Changing Church, which shares with you the vision of a radical, progressive faith, and isn't prepared just to sit back and wait for pontiffs and conclaves and councils to make it all happen (or stop it happening).

I love your ecumenical inclusiveness – which prompts me to tell you what happened at the international ecumenical conference when a man rushed in shouting 'Fire! The building's on fire!'

The Methodists immediately gather in a corner and start a prayer meeting.

The Baptists cry out 'Where's the water?'

The Congregationalists shout 'Everybody for themselves!'

The Presbyterians mumble 'No problem! We are the brands predestined to be plucked from the burning.'

The Fundamentalists bellow 'Flee from the wrath to come! – Matthew 3:7.'

The Salvation Army make a joyful noise, praising God for the blessing fire brings.

The Lutherans nail a notice to the door giving 95 reasons why the fire is not justified.

The Quakers say they will not be moved . . . till moved by the Spirit.

The Unitarians get up . . . and both leave in different directions.

The Roman Catholics form a procession and march out in grand style.

The Anglicans . . . wake up.

The Uniting Church of Australia appoints a chairperson who will in due course arrange for a committee to look into the matter.

But I digress. I have a confession to make (so I guess I've come to the right place!). I am a Quaker, at the humanist end of the Quaker spectrum, and the last time I attended a Catholic Mass was when I was filming on the Falls Road in Belfast in the 70s, during the English Troubles (sometimes referred to by those who don't know their history as the Irish Troubles). I wanted to capture on film the moment when the priest held aloft the Eucharist wafer. As he was about to do so, my cameraman signalled frantically that he had run out of film. I knew it took 20 seconds or so to reload – and this wasn't the kind of situation where I could demand a Take 2. So in a moment of unholy panic I shouted from the back of the church, 'Hold it, Father!' There was a deathly silence. Two hundred heads swivelled round, and four hundred eyes bored into me. But the good man did as he was asked. He held the wafer aloft for 20 seconds, as if in a freeze-frame. The camera was reloaded, I called 'Action!', and we got our film.

So you see, I am not altogether familiar with Catholic ways. When I was kindly invited to give the homily today I had to ask exactly what a homily was! I vaguely remembered that Homily was the name of one of the Borrowers in Mary Norton's novel of that name (fetchingly played by Celia Imre in the film version), but I couldn't quite see how that related to your invitation. In these circumstances you would be forgiven for asking what on earth I'm doing here.

I'm a writer, a broadcaster, and an investigative journalist. My most recent investigative enterprise is a book called *Who on*

Earth was Jesus? It's about the modern quest for the historical Jesus, the human Jesus, Jesus BC. For many years now, scholars and specialist historians have been working to see if it's possible to separate out the carpenter's son in early-first-century Galilee from the iconic Christ of Faith constructed by his late-first-century followers several decades after his death. Can we get behind the theology, the mythology, the power-politics of the early Church, to find the Jesus who wasn't a Christian (because Christianity hadn't been invented), wasn't a Catholic (because the Church hadn't been heard of), and would no doubt have been astonished and dismayed if he had been able to see what the world would make of him and his message?

In *Who on Earth was Jesus?* I look at all the major schools of historical Jesus scholarship, Catholic, Protestant, Jewish and Humanist. There's even a chapter on Joseph Ratzinger's book *Jesus of Nazareth*. There's a great sentence in that book, by the way. Having offered his view of Jesus, the Pope writes: 'Everyone is free to contradict me.' You don't hear that very often from the Episcopal See of Rome – or his representatives in Brisbane!

OK, so there are scholarly views of Jesus to set alongside the pictures we have all grown up with. How does Jesus look when, with the help of specialist historians, we've peeled away the layers of mythology and magic? One very eminent scholar, Marcus Borg, describes it as 'meeting Jesus again – for the first time!'

What comes across most clearly is not so much a 'gentle Jesus meek and mild,' but a rebel Jesus, a rebel with a cause. This Jesus has no time for rules, regulations and commandments imposed by religious or secular law-givers, no time for 'living by the book', no time for legalism. You mustn't do this or that on the Sabbath? 'Rubbish!' says Jesus: 'the Sabbath was made for you, not you for the Sabbath!' All those ritual purity rules? 'Nonsense!' says Jesus, who simply ignores the laws prescribing who you can eat and drink with, whose company you can keep. He liked to party with the riff-raff, the kind of people good religious folk were supposed to steer clear of. He had women friends, and it was rumoured that some of them were no better than they ought to be.

Blessed are the rich and powerful? Blessed are the proud? Blessed are those whose bellies are well filled? Blessed are those who glory in war and conquest? 'Come off it!' says Jesus: 'It's the poor, the powerless, the hungry, the peacemakers, whose full human dignity is to be honoured.' Love your neighbour and honour your father and mother? 'Not good enough!' says Jesus, 'Try loving your enemies!' An eye for an eye and a tooth for a tooth? 'Forget it! Someone threatens you, return a soft answer! Someone hits you, offer the other cheek! *Let us try what love will do!'*

I'll tell you what it will do. It will turn the world upside down. Is that a problem? Only for those who are smugly satisfied that at present it's the right way up.

Something else I've picked up on my investigative quest. Jesus the man, son of Mary and Joseph, charismatic teacher and notorious troublemaker, wasn't just one of those smooth-tongued preachers who had a way with words. Well, he *did* have a way with words – think of those amazing parables, think of the 'sermon on the mount' – but what mattered to Jesus was walking the walk rather than talking the talk. I guess those Galilean villagers in Capernaum and Nazareth and Bethsaida wouldn't have been impressed for long by a do-gooding preacher unless . . . well, unless they saw that he *was* doing good, matching his words with action. Anyone could preach justice and equality. Not everyone who did so was prepared to get their hands dirty, to embrace the leper, to mix with the down and out, to befriend the despised tax collector and the prostitute, and to defy convention by siding openly with a woman caught in the act of adultery. But that was Jesus all over. To hell with the rules: let's put love to the test . . .

For Mercy, Pity, Peace and Love / Is God, our father dear. / And Mercy, Pity, Peace and Love / Is man, his child and care. / For Mercy has a human heart, / Pity a human face, / And Love the human form divine, / And Peace a human dress.

That's how the poet William Blake put it. That's how Jesus lived it.

The scholars I came to admire most as I studied their work and tried to summarise it in basic English, free of theological jargon, were those whose own lives were clearly changed by the subject of their study: Walter Wink, who took his non-violent Jesus to fight apartheid in South Africa; George Wells, the atheist scholar who began by denying that there ever was a historical Jesus, and had the courage to say 'I got it wrong!'; and Bob Funk, founder of the

Jesus Seminar, who challenged the American churches to throw out Jesus the icon and take on board Jesus the iconoclast.

In *Who on Earth was Jesus?* I have a story about John Dominic Crossan, the not-always-orthodox Catholic scholar whose books have been international best-sellers. He tells how he imagines meeting up with the object of his studies.

Jesus tells him, 'I've read your book *The Historical Jesus*, Dominic, and it's quite good. So now are you ready to live by my vision and join me in my programme?'

Crossan answers, 'I don't think I have the courage, Jesus – but I did describe it quite well, didn't I, and the method was especially good, wasn't it?'

'Thank you Dominic,' says Jesus, 'for not falsifying the message to suit your own incapacity. That at least is something.'

'Is it enough?' asks Crossan.

'No, Dominic,' says Jesus, 'it is not.'

David Boulton is a British broadcaster, writer and investigative journalist. Author of 20 books including The Trouble With God *and* Who On Earth Was Jesus? *Member of the religious society of Friends (Quakers), the Sea of Faith Network and the British Humanist Association. He now lectures and runs workshops in Britain, the USA, Canada, Australia and New Zealand.*

I THINK YOU'RE WINNING!

by Marina Aboody Thacker

'I think you're winning!' was the first thing my mother said when she met Fr Peter Kennedy. It was Sunday morning; Peter was standing at the back door of St Mary's farewelling people after Mass. Mum was visiting from interstate and the church was packed compared to Sunday morning back home. It was 2006 and my devout mother was a bit overwhelmed to see so many Catholics in the one place. It was like the 'old days', except none of her seven children were there. Her family were Maronite Christians and had fled the Lebanese–Syrian border to Irish Catholic dominated country New South Wales. 'None of you set foot in a church now,' she announced last Christmas.

'I do, I go to St Mary's every week and sing!' I piped up. I was trying to gain some recognition from her, as usual, amongst the crowd of heterosexuals and their children around the table. 'The Brisbane Lesbian and Gay Pride Choir have been at St Mary's for over ten years now, you know.' Well, that was a Christmas dinner conversation killer, mentioning church and then the 'L' word in the one sentence. It made a few people uncomfortable enough to change the subject straight away! I am so happy to be leading the lesbian and gay choir but I can't say I was 'winning' on the family front.

The St Mary's community had become part of my life since Tony Robertson, a gay Catholic social worker, suggested it would be a great place for the choir to rehearse. We had been at the South Brisbane Bowls Club but we couldn't really afford to stay on there after the first grant ran out. Everyone thought it was a great idea to maintain an inner-city location and so every Tuesday, year after year, there we were in the main church or in the church house singing away for hours. We were right next door to St Vincent's hostel so a few visitors would wander in and watch or sit with us. The homeless, who had set up in the garden outside, also came in for supper and made pleasant comments about how the choir sounded. Once a month we sat around the altar and had a committee meeting after rehearsal.

The choir rehearsed most weeks and performed at about sixteen gigs a year. We sang for book launches, weddings, parties, World AIDS Day, Anti Homophobia Day, the Woodford Folk Festival. We joined with other community choirs for peace rallies, refugee causes and International Year of Older People. We trekked off to Mardi Gras, the bus departing from St Mary's carpark. We signed up for the Choral Festival at the Gay Games and got to sing in the Opera House with gay choirs from around the world. I invited my parents to come to Sydney for the concert and see the community choir I'd been conducting for five years. It was the highlight of my musical career. The choir was very strong, with 28 singers, well prepared and excited for the opportunity to sing in Australia's Opera House. Mum quickly replied, 'No, I hate . . . Sydney!'

Our biggest performance was always Pride Fair Day in June each year at Musgrave Park. We prepared a brand new set of songs every year and sang for our peers on the most exciting day for gay, lesbian, bisexual and transgender people in Brisbane. We visited our sister choirs in Melbourne for the Gay Choral Festival and in Canberra for another big sing, and one year we invited the Canberra Gay and Lesbian Qwire up to sing with us. We planned a concert for the night before Pride Fair Day so we could all march together the next morning and sing in Musgrave Park together afterwards. We offered to billet our visitors and publicise the event as a joint concert in the Brisbane Pride Program. It was a long-term plan and it would replace our annual end-of-year concert. We would also sing a few songs together, so there was much preparation and rehearsing to be done for the 'One Voice' Concert on Friday 13 June 2004.

The week of the concert, I was standing in the newsagent's in West End photocopying music scores when my mobile rang.

It was Fr Terry Fitzpatrick. He was cheerful and calm and enquired how things were going with the concert. I knew St Mary's church office had already received a few complaint calls about the concert being held inside the church. Why, when we have been singing inside the Church for six years? Was it because we were selling tickets? Or having a bar? St Mary's have had concerts before, what's the difference? 'Well Marina, there is possibly a busload of conservative Catholics planning to come down from Maryborough to boycott your event on Friday night. I don't want you to be alarmed but it might be a good idea to notify the police of your concert!' What? What sort of visitors were we getting? 'We've been talking about your concert at the House and we'd like to support the choir and pay for a couple of security guards to keep an eye on things.'

'Homosexual Choir Has Pride of Place in Church' yelled the headlines of the *Courier-Mail*. We hadn't had so much attention in the press since our visit to Toowoomba when the *Chronicle* printed 'Mayor Boos "Sexual" Choir' singing in the Youth Centre. There was no doubt we were alarmed and fearful about the idea of our concert facing a possible boycott. Bishop Bathersby sent a letter to Fr Peter Kennedy requesting he stop the concert from going ahead. Peter never received this letter but read about the instruction in the newspaper. It was the most stressful run-up to a concert I'd ever had. What were we bringing on to St Mary's? The Bishop must have been a little concerned as he took a mini-stroke and ended up in hospital before the Friday. The community of St Mary's were well informed of the conflict and stood with us to go ahead. The Catholic Auxiliary Bishop of Brisbane, Brian Finnegan, on the Friday afternoon before the concert sent a fax to Peter Kennedy saying that since Peter had disobeyed the Archbishop he demanded that the Blessed Sacrament be removed from the church.

Peter was away from Brisbane that night but sent word to say that the Blessed Sacrament was not to be removed from the church. However, others decided that it was probably in our best interests to abide by the Bishop's command. So they took Jesus and put him in the safe with the money! There is no record of Jesus railing against homosexuals but there's plenty of evidence of Jesus railing against money. Word spread further around Brisbane that we were under threat. The Church House was fielding the negative calls and threats of action. We were surrounded by letters, emails, discussions online and the people of St Mary's. The night began with queues of supporters out the door and down the street waiting to get tickets. Cabaret tables had to be removed to let in the numbers. Children had to sit on the floor while many adults stood up the back. We waited until everyone was safely inside and there were no buses sighted by security. You could hear a pin drop. Fr Terry opened our evening and spoke cheerfully and calmly and welcomed the Canberra singers to the night. Jo Justo took over as MC and it was the most extraordinary concert the choir has ever done. We sang extremely well and so did our visitors. The audience were the regular faces of friends and family and GLBT peers but this time there were also wide smiles and cheers from members of St Mary's right there with us.

The choir has singers from all walks of society. The school teachers seem to find it hardest to be 'out' and sing in public. Singers choose each time whether they will perform or not at the gigs. The choir attracts Catholics, non-Catholics, anti-Catholics and lapsed Catholics. Over the years we have had two ex-priests, one ex–Christian brother, one ex-nun and two men who left the seminary before completing. Singers in the choir are members of the Catholic support group for gays and lesbians called Acceptance. It was extremely important to these singers that their community choir was making its home inside their place of worship, something never heard of before. On the other hand, it was also often discussed amongst singers that we should not be here as we had two ritual abuse survivors who found it creepy to come back inside a church each week. We debated whether it was appropriate to stay or move to a non-religious venue. The objectors to staying, whilst struggling with their memory of life involved with religion, agreed it wasn't too bad to put up with St Mary's since it was such an extraordinary community of people.

Each year we hunted down another venue to hold our annual concert. We rang the Anglican Church in South Brisbane to make a booking for late November one year and upon announcing our name, the woman's voice requested, 'Can you hold for one moment please . . .' She came back and said 'No, we can't rent you the hall; we are not allowed to.' We discovered through the Anti-discrimination Board that non-profit community organisations were allowed to discrimate against anyone they chose to!

Discussions to stay or go continually challenged us as new members came and went. Various singers searched for a rehearsal space that could possibly offer us what St Mary's did, forty weeks a year. Both the house and the church were made available to us for minimal rent or donation. We had access to a grand piano, large space inside the church as the chairs were all placed around the edges, off-street parking, lighting, safety, the occasional gig held in the church like Swoon In June or World AIDS Day and a group of people committed to equality and social justice around us. That's what we were singing about.

St Mary's was always in the paper. For some weeks it was daily at the height of the conflict between Peter and the Archbishop. Some singers were thinking what could we do in support of this terrible situation. The St Mary's community were now under threat of losing their venue, their home. We talked about it in the break at choir. 'We should offer to sing for St Mary's to show we support them.' 'Yes, that's a good idea, let's make contact and offer a few dates to Peter and Terry.' At this time we came to hear of the Treaty Ceremony that was going to be held at the end of the year; it was to be a cultural event with an indigenous smoking. I thought we needed a special song for this occasion and we should ask other choirs to join us as we might be losing our home as well as the community of St Mary's losing theirs.

I just had to arrange the Australian song 'House of Love' by Wayne Burt into four-part harmony. It summed up St Mary's for me in music. Most singers looked forward to the event. Others remained silent at rehearsal but behind the scenes there was discussion, disagreement, discontent and one night at last the silence was broken. 'We should move out of St Mary's, this is not our battle.' 'I'm sick of seeing St Mary's in the paper, I just want to go somewhere where we can sing.' 'This whole situation is stressing me out each week, I don't know what is going to happen, or where rehearsal is going to be, I've decided to leave the choir.' 'Marina, I don't agree with Peter Kennedy, I'm going to resign.' There was a reluctance to spend any rehearsal time on solving the problem. We had a gig next week, we have to practise! For some time the cracks in the choir's fabric grew wider. 'We should have left some time ago.' 'We should not be connected to a religious building. We should just find somewhere commercial and pay proper rent and be independent.' These voices had no loyalty, respect, sentimentality, appreciation or concern for the community of St Mary's. The chair of the choir announced we would spend one hour on discussing the issues at rehearsal. As the paid employee of the choir, I have no voting rights and so offered to chair the discussion. The night arrived and I had come to realise that, 'There was no way I was able to chair the meeting that night because I felt so strongly about the choir and St Mary's – someone else would have to do it.' An ex-committee member stepped up and we went ahead. That night we decided to indefinitely move out of St Mary's until we had further discussions. We would rehearse down the road to take the pressure off and to ensure we didn't lose any rehearsal time with the sit-ins planned at the church.

It was a standoff. I found many people did not speak up. We had accepted the support and comfort of unconditional security from a community who were now certainly going to lose their location. How could we think of moving out to a non-active, apolitical, peaceful venue that charged high rent and asked no questions? What? Were you here when the security guards stood at the door of our concert? When the Catholics with a social justice conscience paid to see us? We have stored our costumes and library in the loft, we have rehearsed and workshopped through weekends and borrowed equipment. We have been trusted and respected actively, not in a tolerant kind of way that just lets us exist. This community has extended both arms to help us, promote us, encourage us and we have singers practising in this community. Where are you now? Why aren't you speaking up? Catholics and non-Catholics, anti-religious and other religions speak now. It's not OK to accept what we have for years and years and then be complacent at a desperate time for this community. You can't possibly think you joined the gay and lesbian choir to sing proudly and be invisible every other moment. Gay and Lesbian anything is political as soon as you step outside your front door.

Another discussion was planned, a limited time set. We heard speakers for and against. The singers against St Mary's sat together. Gently and carefully the singers who spoke in support of St Mary's came forward and in their own way gave back exactly what St Mary's had given us all over the years: a quiet strength to be exactly who we are with dignity. This is not the time at all to go. The ship is sinking for sure but we will not jump out while there is a community to stand beside. Two members left the choir that night, unhappy with the decision to stay.

A new member joined. Fr Peter Kennedy is in trouble, one singer explained. Why's that? 'Because he won't put a dress on!' Hey?

The Brisbane Gay and Lesbian Pride Choir called St Mary's home for over 11 years. We decided to move out at the same time as the original St Mary's community moved out. It pleased the anti-religious in our group and the St Mary's supporters at the same time. We are now based at the Old Brisbane Museum in Windsor where we can't be heard over the orchestras in the building!!

When St Mary's were offered to move down the road to the Trades and Labour Council Building, the Combined Unions Choir who are based there were delighted. They quickly offered to sing the St Marys-in-Exile into the building on Sunday morning. I have also been conducting this choir of unionists, social justice and peace activists for twelve years. They jumped at the opportunity, as did the Queensland Council of Unions to offer some support for a community that is much broader in its thinking than a religious formula.

The phone rang weeks after we left. 'You better not go to the media and say you have been kicked out,' a voice said. 'Why would I do that, when it's not true?' I replied. I suspect the voice was a conservative gay Catholic who wanted us to stay and be part of what was left in the empty white building.

After conducting the Brisbane Lesbian and Gay Pride Choir for ten years, I invited my parents again to come and hear us sing. It was the launch of our tenth year, to be held at Government House in Bardon. A silver-tipped envelope arrived in their country letterbox from Her Excellency, Quentin Bryce and to my surprise they accepted! They stood on the perfect lawn, like statues in their best clothes, looking at interactions around them . . . singers chatting with their guests, Tony Robertson in his camp red kilt and me grasshoppering from one singer to another. My children were there too with their donor grandparents, and my daughter kept saying 'Sitti [Lebanese for Grandmother], we're going to meet the Queen of Queensland, you know!' With immaculate timing two special guests arrived: Peter and Terry came down the stairs into the garden and surrounded my parents with the familiarity they needed to get through their first gay event led by their daughter. And of course the singing was magnificent.

Marina Aboody Thacker ran out of the Queensland Conservatorium of Music in 1986 with a music degree in her hand. She was racing to get away from classical music and into the real world of Community Arts, Community Theatre and most of all Community Choirs. This has been her passion since then.

Marina has conducted many singers from many different communities including the Victorian Trade Union Choir, Brisbane Combined Unions Choir, The West End Women's Chorus, Coro Abruzzo, Brisbane City Council Multicultural Choir and the African Women's Chorus. She is the founding Musical Director of the Brisbane Lesbian and Gay Pride Choir and led the choir in their first original stage musical The Letter Q *in 2009. Marina sang with the Petit Four quartet for many years and now teaches music in primary schools on the southside of Brisbane.*

BEYOND THE CREEDS: REFLECTIONS OF A PROTESTANT CATHOLIC

by Noel Preston

The imposing Catholic church on the corner of Peel and Merivale Streets, South Brisbane (St Mary's) was a fascinating part of the local geography in my boyhood, long before I ever met Peter Kennedy. I was raised a Methodist and, indeed, my father was the Methodist minister in the West End and South Brisbane area from 1948 to 1963, in days when Catholics and Protestants rarely met and viewed each other with suspicion. My father's brand of Methodism was progressive in its time. He exercised a high-profile, public ministry, majoring on community outreach including several highly successful community service initiatives and gathered a large congregation of all comers from the far corners of fifties Brisbane. As a boy in the 1950s the heritage-listed St Mary's, with its formidable but now demolished convent in Peel Street, was a familiar landmark. I often passed by, wondering what the mysterious and powerful Irish sect gathering there was up to, with no imagination that one day this place would house a local Christian community with which I would affiliate.

I returned to live in West End in 1982 at a time of significant change in my own life. Indeed the changes were largely shaped by the Joh (Bjelke-Petersen) years in the 1970s through Christian social activism, accompanying my role in the ecumenical group, Action for World Development. Though I was a Uniting Church minister, Catholic spirituality and social justice teaching had been imprinted on my mid-life development via this engagement. That was when I first met Peter Kennedy who soon became a mentor and friend, just as he has been a compassionate guide to hundreds who were making difficult and painful life transitions. Peter's hospitality and gentle non-directive spiritual guidance provided me with re-creative spiritual experiences first at his Mt Tamborine retreat and subsequently at Sallywattle in the Numinbah Valley.

On the weekends at Mass in St Mary's I found many of my colleagues from the ecumenical activism of the 1970s, who had gravitated to St Mary's partly because they were somewhat isolated in their mainstream parishes. There were always a few non-Catholics in the congregation including some like me who were ordained Protestant clergy, but who found St Mary's spoke to their need for an authentic faith. We shared a profound affinity with the liturgy practised at St Mary's. We were also drawn to the way St Mary's served as a vanguard of progressive Christianity, sometimes in tension with the wider church communion to which it was connected, just as my father's Methodist church just a few blocks away in West End had been in an earlier era, or so it felt to me.

I came to appreciate how the St Mary's community not only encouraged and supported many social-justice initiatives, but also how it practised inclusiveness in a community whose company includes many who are excluded from communion with the Roman church like divorcees, married priests, gay and lesbian people and others with stories of suffering. The hallmark of this community led by Fathers Peter and Terry was empowerment of those exploring the boundaries of belief, and alongside that, cultivating multi-faceted services to the poor through the Micah Project. Though there was always a passing crowd in the congregation, since the early nineties a consolidated community emerged which identified itself as a controversial and prophetic agency, faithful to the core intent of the Gospel, experimental in its participatory liturgy, daring in what was said from its pulpit and encouraging those who attended to explore a deep and meditative spirituality. Despite a certain ecclesiastical messiness at times (or perhaps because of it) and a naivete, sometimes unaware of its subversiveness, a direction had been set so that St Mary's was the place in Brisbane which stood out as a beacon of credibility, authenticity and relevance challenging the rest of the archdiocese and the wider Christian communion; that is, it signified a different future for the church.

I quickly came to regard myself as part of the loosely connected St Mary's community. This was now my primary spiritual home, though I continued to participate in other faith communities, sometimes in my capacity as a Uniting Church minister. There was one particular occasion when it dawned on me that I had moved beyond being a visitor/participant at St Mary's. One Sunday morning in Advent 1989 I attended St Mary's in the knowledge that the next day I was to undergo urgent and major surgery for bowel cancer. As I stood around the eucharistic table with hundreds of communicants, I was overwhelmed by a grief I did not fully understand, and then a sense of quiet settled in me as I realised that I belonged to this community more than to any other faith community. Many times since I have preached at St Mary's, acted as a eucharistic minister, exercised pastoral care in the community and been on its leadership team, and yet, I remain too Protestant, or shall I say too non-denominational, to have formally become a Roman Catholic. Now, since St Mary's has been forced into exile, cut off from communion with Rome's bishops, the choice to be Protestant Catholics, or even perhaps to be 'post-Christian', is now the choice that is being embraced by the St Mary's community as a whole.

My personal disenchantment with 'Rome', reinforced as it was for years from the pulpit at St Mary's, is deep-seated. The Catholicism which I first warmly encountered through Action for World Development in the 1970s was invigorated by the Vatican Council initiated by the reforming Pope John XXIII. However, under the pontificate of John Paul II, the Vatican, which makes the spurious dual claim to be a political state as well as the See of the Vicar of Christ, lost much of that reforming zeal. Throughout the twenty-six years John Paul II was pope, the Vatican contributed to social justice in some parts of the world but overall it remained a very conservatising force within the Church, alienating and oppressing many, including women and homosexual persons, while rendering exclusion on some of the finest theological visionaries like the American ethicist Charles Curran and the Latin American Leonardo Boff.

Nonetheless, official Catholic teaching, even that sanctioned by the present Pope in his former capacity as doctrinal gatekeeper, retains a cutting edge which calls for urgent remedies to the stark inequalities between developed and developing countries, inequalities stoked also by various forms of exploitation, oppression and corruption. However, Pope John Paul II and his successor, both men of considerable scholarship, have imposed the views of the Vatican on many bioethical and sexuality issues in ways I cannot accept. Those views are informed by dogmatic absolutism and a rigid natural law position which eschews a contextual approach to ethical decision-making. John Paul II's papacy was marked by the stark contradiction between his tardiness in dealing with the grotesque behaviour of paedophile priests and his harsh judgments about the sexual behaviour of the laity, including a policy denouncing the use of condoms, even for those suffering from AIDS, thereby condemning millions to an unnecessary death.

As a Uniting Church minister, albeit one on the boundary of my own ecclesial communion (for I had no appointment in the UCA from 1981 to 2001, a period in which I worked as an academic in secular universities), I have had the privilege of exploring the boundaries of belief and the practice of spirituality without the constraints subtly imposed by institutional religion. During these years, association with St Mary's and its pulpit provided the space and the inspiration alongside my academic work in ethics to form a view about both the tradition from which I had come and also a vision about the kind of spirituality and faith which made sense for the 21st century.

My appreciation of Catholicism at its best is such that I see that tradition as much more likely to give birth to credible and relevant religious forms and beliefs than the churches historically linked to the Reformation. Those denominations are now, by and large, historical relics. From the vantage of St Mary's I formed the view that the future of their Australian offspring, the Uniting Church, depends on its capacity to go beyond that history and much of the theology that the Reformers emphasised. Though the Uniting Church in Australia contains elements within it that are comfortable in making such a journey beyond the boundaries of orthodox belief, there are also many within its ranks who cling fundamentally to outmoded packages of belief and practice. I conclude that its ageing demography and the theological ambiguities the UCA embraces mean that, at best, this important Australian experiment in ecumenism is but a bridge to 'deep ecumenism', which goes beyond the boundaries of Christianity and which might transform church buildings and programs into 'spirituality spaces' with a broader agenda.

In my case, the context of progressive Catholicism provided me with the stimulation and support for this journey. Not only is the contemplative spirituality nurtured in Catholicism for centuries an abiding gift but also there is an intellectual dimension in the catholic (or universal) stance which, on one hand, finds fundamentalism alien while, on the other, spawns creative and innovative theological thinking that welcomes engagement across the disciplines of knowledge. So it is that Catholic writers like Rosemary Radford Reuther, Leonardo Boff, Thomas Berry, Diarmuid O'Murchu and Paul Collins have informed and inspired me in embracing an eco-theology appropriate in the 21st century.

But this approach is a world apart from the orthodoxy defined by the Vatican and many other church hierarchies. Pope John Paul II and then Cardinal Ratzinger, now Pope Benedict XVI, are in a line of succession which has used doctrinal and liturgical orthodoxy as a weapon of control. This style has been characteristic of many forms of institutional religion over the ages including Protestant evangelical fundamentalists. They practise what I call 'creedalism', which feeds off the powerful need we humans have for certainty and control in the face of uncertainty and vulnerability. Historically, the classical creeds of Christendom, like the Apostle's and Nicene Creeds, have been used to sort out the theologically correct sheep from the incorrect goats and, thereby, to buttress audacious claims about authority on divine truth and decrees which broker communion with the divine.

As long as the cosmology and worldview which the creedal game assumed held together, that authority survived. But that is no longer the case. As Einstein showed us, we live in a universe of relativities rather than absolutes. On the one hand contemporary scientific understandings of the universe and the evolution of life dramatically differ from those which held sway in biblical times or in the medieval worldview so foundational in fashioning orthodox religious discourse in Christendom. Also, contemporary social science has demonstrated that religions are culture-bound. Indeed, notwithstanding claims about revelation, what is clear is that religious dogma, creeds and theology are fallible human constructions. Moreover they tend to literalise and ossify the metaphorical and mythic accounts which point to truths beyond the words which are used. Creeds and theological formulae are therefore amenable to reinterpretation and new explanations. Perhaps the Johannine affirmation 'God is Love' is creed enough and the Gospel injunction to 'love your neighbour', the bottom-line in ethical guidance. In saying that, I am not advocating theological revisions which will remove the divine mystery or release us from the challenge to live ethically. Of course, there are limits to how much revision of the creeds can be undertaken while still retaining a meaningful identification with one's religious tradition: it's becoming harder than ever to put new wine into old (religious) wineskins.

Years ago some of us foresaw the inevitable outcome of the St Mary's experiment. A community that has broken with the authority forged in the Constantinian accord of the fourth century CE, and which regarded denominational allegiances as peripheral and was increasingly at home with the idea of religionless Christianity or even a post-Christian spirituality – such a community of faith has crossed over to become part of a growing movement of humanity that puts more emphasis on following the way of Jesus rather than believing certain things about Jesus. For this movement, of which St Mary's-in-Exile is clearly a significant part, even the Jesus story must be bracketed within a commitment to preserve life on this planet and transcend our anthropocentric delusions.

Noel Preston is an ethicist, theologian and social commentator, currently Adjunct Professor in the Key Centre for Ethics, Law Justice and Governance, Griffith University. He retired in November 2004 as the founding Director of the Unitingcare Centre for Social Justice. He is currently a Member of the Advisory Panel of Green Cross Australia and the Committee of Earth Charter Australia. He is a regular public commentator on social ethics, though in retirement he is particularly researching eco-theology and eco-spirituality. Among seven books he has sole or co- authored and edited, his introductory textbook Understanding Ethics *was reissued as a revised third edition in late 2007 with major additions and updates. In 2007 he also edited and contributed to an issue of the journal* Social Alternatives *themed 'Global Ethics'. In 2004 he was made a Member of the Order of Australia for services to the community in the field of ethics.*

FAITH, COMMUNITY AND TRADITION

by M. Anne Brown

As I grapple with what the experience of St Mary's 'exile' and the period leading up to that mean to me, a few things stand out. These are what I would like to offer to others – those who are also part of St Mary's now or at some other time, or who have come across this story through sometimes quite strange accounts in the media or elsewhere. Because I am still caught in the afterwash of all these events I may not sense their deeper resonances very clearly; I am making my way through it all. Although I've talked with others about developments and feelings throughout the passage of the last year, this is simply a reflection on what these events mean for me, brought together as they sit at present. I write here from my own experiences and traditions. I don't wish particularly to glorify St Mary's, but I am reflecting on some of the ways in which it is and has been significant for me – and these are profound. Nor are these remarks intended to be comparative – I am not saying that particular qualities are to be found only at St Mary's and not in other places, but simply reflecting on my experience there, as an ordinary member of that community since the early 1990s.

The threads that stand out for me, all interwoven, are St Mary's as a place where you can bring your search for what is most fundamental and most intimate in life, as a place of faith, as community, and as part of the living tradition of Catholicism.

St Mary's has been and is for me a place of respect and mutuality. There is an atmosphere of taking people seriously, of acknowledging people, of respect that is not contingent upon particular ways of expressing belief. This acknowledgement is a subtle and unselfconscious thing, an ordinary and unpolished thing. It flows into and out from the shared prayer of Mass. This does not mean that members of the congregation are constantly seeking to express themselves or that there is any pressure to do so, but simply that a sense of openness and mutuality has grown over time. Nor does acknowledgement imply any need to agree with everything that is said, including by the homilists – far from it. It means that I feel, and others I know feel, that we could talk about things close to us, that are part of our search for what is at the heart of life, or that press in on us, and that it is likely that someone will be listening and trying to make sense of what is heard.

Many things contribute to making this atmosphere – the warmth and openness of various people in the congregation, the complexity of the congregation as a gathering of people from many different walks of life, age groups and experiences, the range of activities that the community has engaged in over the years, from longstanding social-justice programs to prayer meetings, scripture reflections, meditation groups, liturgical dance groups, social gatherings and so on. But one of the fundamental factors underpinning this practice of acknowledgement draws from the two priests, Fathers Peter Kennedy and Terry Fitzpatrick, themselves. I don't want to dwell on Peter and Terry, but both have been and are vital to the life of the community; they are the leaders of the community and its priests. You could say that Peter is in many ways an ordinary bloke, even an ordinary bloke with some 'issues', like most of us – but he is an ordinary bloke with issues who is clearly seeking to live deeply in God, or however one can articulate this fundamental experience of being. There is something powerfully honest about Peter's presence as a slightly grumpy old bloke who is deeply motivated by and struggling with a sense of the sacredness and mystery of people and of existence.

Peter and Terry and many members of the congregation work or spend time with, or are themselves, people who have been pushed outside the circles of conventional respect, or who have experienced some form of profound exclusion within the Catholic Church itself or more generally: the mentally ill, prisoners, homeless people, refugees, people who have been abused or dispossessed, homosexuals, simply the frail or isolated or distraught. These interactions can sometimes open a door to a deeper experience of mutuality and what can be a searching, uncomfortable recognition of people's humanity – one that can suddenly make clear the prevailing norms of exchange and their preoccupation with hierarchy and success and turn them on their heads. Increasingly, Indigenous members of the congregation welcome us to country as Mass opens, inviting us all into the sacredness of this exchange through recognition of thousands of generations of Indigenous spiritual practice and insight in this place and into some sense of a different binding of people and place. They bring not only a history of dispossession and survival, but through this welcome offer a powerful testimony to generosity and inclusion. These experiences of the congregation flow into and shape something of the way that community life, but also the Mass itself, takes place. There is a simple kindness and openness towards people that the community has created over time, and that it cherishes.

We bring to Mass our search for understanding, as one of the opening prayers says. We bring our differences, our difficulties, our efforts to engage more deeply with the sources of life. We bring the cycles of life – our romances, weddings and children, our friends and parents, life passages and funerals. We bring our struggles with disappointment, failure, death, the painful recognition of the harm that people do each other, collectively and individually, and the conundrum of what to do in the face of that recognition. We search for what the Mass makes of these and other questions which pull at our lives, and we take part in its remaking of experience and meaning, listening to the stories that we might have lived with since childhood, resonating through our changing experience and understanding, trying to grasp the actions, gestures, words that trace out consecration, communion and blessing, that make the journey through death and resurrection, creation and incarnation, for the doors that they might open in the world.

As lives and sacraments speak to and interweave with each other, people can come to different ways of expressing what elements of faith or of tradition mean to them. This (I suspect) happens across the Church – I certainly know of many examples – but mostly people keep it to themselves. My now deceased elderly mother (along with my brother and sister-in-law), for example, introduced me to St Mary's. She was a devout practising Catholic her entire life; nevertheless her life experiences and her great faith led her to ways of understanding elements of tradition and liturgy that were quite different from what she would have learnt in primary school. She only occasionally alluded to this, but in clear and strong expressions of her understanding. Such differences from the catechism are not unusual, I suspect, including among people who would consider themselves traditional, conventional Catholics (as my mother would have thought of herself). Because there is space for this to be acknowledged at St Mary's the experience of Mass for me, but I think also for others (including my mother during her life), is subtly altered. There is a deeper invitation to enter the intimate conversation between world and sacrament. For my mother, this was a liberation and a homecoming – not a deviation from doctrine, but something that freed her to enter into this living, breathing tradition of spiritual practice and engagement with life as herself, without pretence.

Raising questions about the nature of divinity, the literalness of resurrection, the meaning of virgin birth and so on can seem to be abandoning faith, but it need not be. Faith is not essentially a recitation of dogma; whatever else it might involve, faith surely turns around willingness to be open to and to reach out to life, to keep looking for God or turning to Christ, to keep holding to compassion in the face of defeat, despair, or confusion. One of the messages of the Gospels must be Christ's transcendent response of compassion in the face of ignorance, expediency and violence, a response that turns on its head what seems, in the crucifixion, to be utter defeat, exclusion and humiliation, and that opens the door to life. For me the pathway and the practices of that reaching out to life and compassion spring from the rich spiritual tradition of Catholicism, the deep truths come in that language, not as the only pathway or language but as the one that has shaped me, refreshed at times by reminders, insights or practices from other traditions (such as other meditative traditions).

In thinking about the doctrinal dimensions of our faith, we have become caught in a rigid polarity. It sometimes seems that we are asked to see elements of faith as literally true, in what seems a highly reductionist sense, where 'facts' are increasingly required to be objectively validated. (To require empirical factuality of all dimensions of faith seems to lead more to magic and primitive versions of fundamentalism than to systematic knowledge or to science, if these goals are thought to be desirable by those concerned with doctrinal order.) What in this literal reading does the consecration mean? This is not to assert that tenets of faith are or are not literally true, but to say that preoccupation with this question seems to miss the point of journeys of faith. Alternatively, if a narrowly literalist approach is rejected then it seems we are left with elements of faith as merely representational or symbolic, like a flag or a poster, again understood in a thin sense that is emptied out of any ability to articulate or point to the deeper experiences of being alive in the world. We are left then without language. I don't know how to speak about elements of faith or spiritual truth outside this damaging dichotomy, but I worry that this hollow 'choice' is driving people away from the living roots of our spiritual practice, and rendering them unintelligible.

Certainly this limited and narrow way of attempting to talk about how we understand God or the place of Christ in our lives contributed to the polarisation of debate that was evident in the media representations and interviews leading up to St Mary's 'exile'. What is left are fundamentally misleading representations of positions that have lost their capacity to connect with the deeply experienced truths of people's efforts to live together in God, or to care for each other and the world. Perhaps we could talk also of a sacramental truth, or a truth that is neither simply literal nor merely symbolic but which gestures to fundamental, generative, loving action. Or the dichotomies can be undermined more subversively by humour, for example, when Peter gives one of his whimsical, hilarious and strangely insightful accounts of being a priest in contemporary Australia.

When I first heard of the letter from the Archbishop to Father Peter, and when it first seemed possible that Peter, or the congregation, could be excluded from the diocese, I felt no automatic reaction that I would naturally follow St Mary's into exile, if that were to be the path or the choice ahead. I am a Catholic and am part of the Catholic community. It is an ancient and global community that gives shape and voice to my spiritual path; Scottish Celts among my ancestors may well have suffered real danger to uphold their religion, and at a personal level I have had the good fortune to have felt nurtured in spiritual, emotional and concrete terms by this broader Catholic community at some key points in my life (including but certainly not only at St Mary's). More fundamentally I have no interest in starting or being part of a new, breakaway denomination – nor is that how I think the congregation at St Mary's now see themselves.

The experience of the growing friction between the Archbishop and St Mary's was instructive for me in a number of ways. It was a time of grief for me, and for many others, as we watched the progressive polarisation and failure of communication between the parties – despite what were certainly efforts on the community's part and perhaps also from elsewhere. Sadly, this is a very familiar dynamic in conflict situations. Despite this grief and despite distress at what at least seemed like the lack of respect for the community shown by the apparent inability of diocesan representatives to speak with us, however, it was not these responses that stand out for me. Rather it was my gradual realisation of the importance of the community of St Mary's and my history there. The strength and clarity of this realisation caught me by surprise.

I have for many years thought that community was important; nevertheless, given other obligations I am not a particularly active member of St Mary's; I am not particularly sociable; I'd be hard pressed to remember lots of names. This was not a realisation about community as social connection, despite the real value of that. There was no pressure to go 'into exile' that I was conscious of, so this is not a comment about the conformist elements of community. At the same time, being part of the broader Catholic community is essentially beyond question for me: it is simply the reality. There are other parishes, much closer to where I live than St Mary's, where I could take part in Mass. Nor, however, could I step away from this congregation with whom I have shared Mass for so many years, where I and my brother and sister and other family buried my mother, and where a real part of the concrete reality of my spiritual life has taken place, when that stepping away is implicitly structured as a rejection of the validity of that sharing of Mass and life.

The diocese apparently offered members of the congregation a choice – but for me, and perhaps for many others, that choice was not real. We remain both one thing and the other. To choose either one or the other would be in some sense a lie. We are then in an uncomfortable, but I hope ultimately creative, place. Some people for whom I have great respect and affection could not come to join the congregation in exile; I miss them but am entirely accepting of their action. For them, this delicate balance of belonging, integrity and spiritual vitality (not pitting one against the other but a mix of all these things) had different elements, which made their pathway a true one. Others in the congregation in exile may feel that they have indeed stepped away from the larger Catholic community. These directions are not simply 'choices', as if one could re-arrange at will the meanings that things carry.

There is something important here I feel about the complexity of community, its significance beyond social networks and social rootedness, and the relationship between community and integrity. I don't really know what to make of this. Perhaps, however, part of its significance is that spiritual life is often seen as an individual enterprise, and of course in some important ways it is, but it is also a shared journey, that holds us together with all others. This has a concrete, and not only a noumenous, reality. The importance of our boundaries and the need to patrol them eases as we accept ourselves and come to understand each other better. We do not exist fundamentally independently of each other – this is primarily a spiritual rather than a pragmatic truth; nor is spiritual existence simply an abstract set of ideals or principles but the concrete, embodied experience of life. Together, and over time, we make a place where people become kind to each other, where people reflect on the mysteries of Mass in the suffering and joys of their lives, where people accept and perhaps enter into each others' differences; we carry this and bring to this all the dimensions and places of our lives. We learn this from the liturgy, from the priests, from our practice, but also from each other, in small and large ways. This is the living water of faith and tradition about which the psalmists sing.

(Margaret) Anne Brown works as a Peace and Conflict Studies researcher, currently at the Australian Centre for Peace and Conflict Studies, University of Queensland, from where she is conducting research and practice work in East Timor and Vanuatu. Her research and practice focuses on working with questions of community, conflict and violence across cultural and other division and she has written on human rights, peace-building, East Timor and the Pacific

Islands, among other things. She was born and grew up in Brisbane then worked as a diplomat and lived in different places within Australia and in China for approximately 10 years. She has been a member of the St Mary's congregation, where her brother and sister-in-law also attend, since returning to Brisbane in the early 1990s.

IF ONE IS BOLD ENOUGH TO PREACH, ONE IS MORALLY BOUND TO PREACH INCLUSIVELY

by Peter Norden

I first met Fr Peter Kennedy more than 20 years ago, when he was the prison chaplain at Boggo Road prison in Brisbane and I held the equivalent position at Pentridge prison in Melbourne.

My lasting impression from those first meetings was that he was a very compassionate man, committed to his priestly ministry, creative in his pastoral responses, and engaging in his manner.

Many of the prison chaplains who attended our national gatherings held every two years were of a different nature. Some seemed largely focused on their obligations to simply provide the sacraments to those whose freedom had been taken away from them. Many showed little evidence of their concern for issues of justice and human rights. Some controlled their prison ministry very tightly, allowing only religious sisters or brothers to play a role. Others encouraged a wider involvement by members of the broader Christian community, as liturgists, catechists, counsellors or as friendly visitors.

Peter Kennedy struck me as having a broader view of ministry, beyond the purely ritualistic or strictly sacramental. His model of priestly ministry included an interest in the whole person and he saw the Church as being a key defender of the rights and the dignity of those whom society had judged as criminal.

Peter and those he worked with in Catholic Prison Ministry were not fearful of speaking out, of acting as advocates in the face of injustice.

It is not easy to do this as a prison chaplain. You can find yourself facing closed doors and lack of cooperation from the prison authorities. The chaplains from the other Christian denominations can also step aside from you too, fearful of being associated with a troublemaker, in a work environment that epitomises social control.

You get a sense of the style of Christian ministry when you walk around the prison yards with another chaplain – how much at ease the person is, whom he or she stops to talk to, who reaches out to say hello, and what sort of issues they raise.

Peter Kennedy, as prison chaplain, expressed the three vital aspects of most authentic Christian ministry: priest, pastor and prophet.

I failed to keep contact with Peter after I retired from direct full-time prison ministry almost twenty years ago now. But from time to time, I heard of his inner-city ministry at St Mary's and his work at his country retreat outside of Brisbane. I always felt that he was a kindred spirit, and I celebrated and rejoiced at the effectiveness of his ministry as a fellow priest.

Only in the last twelve months have I re-established communication with him, when I heard of some of the opposition he had encountered from fringe members of the Catholic Church, and more recently from the formal church authorities.

From what I had learnt, there are three areas that have brought criticism towards Peter and his ministry at St Mary's, and they each seem to speak about inclusion, as against exclusion.

Firstly, that he on occasions allowed a woman to preach at Sunday Mass; secondly, that he was prepared to bless the committed relationship of a same-sex couple; and thirdly, that he introduced some inclusive language into the prayers or the ritual blessings of the Church.

None of these things appeared to me to be 'mortally sinful'! Each of the practices appeared to come from a deep-seated commitment to faithful ministry. Finally, I would imagine that there are hundreds of Catholic priests in active ministry around Australia today who would have done the same or similar things, when they recognised that the pastoral situation required it.

The disturbing thing about the complaints brought against Fr Peter Kennedy is that the matters that have been identified can be seen to be aspects of what I would describe as the inclusive nature of his priestly ministry and pastoral practices.

Now who would object to this type of priestly behaviour? People, I suggest, who believe that the church and its membership is some sort of exclusive club. People, I imagine, who would like the doors of the church to be closed to all except the righteous ones. People, I suspect, who believe that they have a sort of ownership of the church themselves, not because of any formal position or hierarchical authority like priesthood or being consecrated as a bishop and so on, but because they believe that the church is theirs and that 'outsiders' are not really welcome, especially those who do not keep the rules.

Peter Kennedy would have experienced this during his time as prison chaplain . . . 'Good Catholic people' believing, and sometimes even being prepared to articulate their belief, 'that you are wasting your time with those criminal types'.

I have also had some experience of Catholic people who take that sort of possessive, controlling approach to their local parish church. They were happy for the church building itself to be closed during the day, as long as they knew the secret side entrance, or had their own key to get inside. They objected to the students from our parish primary school having access to the church during the week, on one occasion referring to them as 'heathens', because some did not come from Catholic families.

Two so-called 'pillars of the church', the sacristan and the choir leader, secretly put forward formal objections to the parish school extension building plans before the local government authority, because they had an insatiable fear that their church would be closed and taken over for school use. In doing so they caused months of delay, preventing the completion of the school extension by the beginning of the school year. So much for their Christian commitment of service to the disadvantaged students and families of the parish school!

People who come into a Sunday worship service intent on taking notes about minutiae of liturgical practice, with pen and paper in hand, generally have a small head and a small heart. They see the Church as some sort of club, with rules, and authentic membership can be tested by one's rigid conformity to those rules and regulations, no matter how inconsequential those rules may appear.

I recall at one of our Youth Liturgies at St Ignatius Church in Richmond, where at the time more than 200 young people would attend on the first Sunday afternoon of each month, that one of the visiting parents raised more than 20 objections to the way the liturgy proceeded! She could not have had much time for prayer or joyful worship in companionship with the others gathered there.

One of the objections was that the homily was given by a young person, not the celebrant of the Mass. Actually, I was prepared for that one, and always gave the homily myself, immediately after the Gospel, even if it was a very short one, sometimes only one or two minutes. The address then given by the young person I always identified as a reflection, to avoid the 'liturgical police' who might have been in the congregation!

Of course, many of the young people who came to the Mass came because they wanted to hear the young person's reflections on his or her journey of faith. I am sure the same situation was true for those who shared the homily over the years at St Mary's Church in South Brisbane.

There never seemed to be any objection when the homily space was taken by one of the many appeals for money for one cause or another.

This incident reminds me of the comments made by another 'pillar of the church' soon after the introduction of these regular youth Masses, a monthly liturgy that had been proving very successful. I was asked: why are we doing all this for young people? We should be providing more services for the elderly of the parish! I was amazed at this comment, noting that it was very rare in most Catholic parishes around Australia to see anyone between the ages of fifteen and twenty-five.

When spies come into a parish faith community intent on taking notes or reporting the parish, or the priest in particular, to the church authorities, it is a test of the authenticity of leadership in the Church. How do you respond? It is impossible for an authority in Rome to respond appropriately. It is a responsibility that must be faced by the local church diocesan leadership. It seems to me that the form of behaviour and the approach and attitude of such people intent on making complaints is lacking essential Christian values. They need to be treated with care and concern, but they should not be given credence or allowed to assume authority that their behaviour does not warrant.

Why is it that they remain anonymous? Do they ever speak directly to the person against whom the complaint is laid? Do they have any sense at all of the damage they cause: to the church minister, to the local church community, to the wider community?

It is not an easy situation for the local diocesan church authority to deal with, but the faith community should not become the victim as a result of such secretive, dubious and undermining behaviour.

Traditionally, over the centuries, church authorities have given credence to the 'vox populi', the voice of the people, or that of the wider general congregation. This should not easily be ignored. Why is it that individuals, acting in secret, can be given such authority? Is this sort of behaviour reinforced by giving them such credence? Can we expect more of such behaviour in the future? Will they become even more insistent, given their apparent 'success' on this occasion?

I recall being a resident priest in St Ignatius Parish in Richmond in inner-city Melbourne where for more than ten years senior students from Loreto Mandeville Hall had attended the Sunday morning service and then had accompanied local members of the congregation in visiting the sick at the nearby Epworth Hospital. The Year 12 students were all volunteers and many continued as volunteers after they completed their final-year studies.

Some weeks there were fewer students in attendance, especially if it was near examination time or during school mid-year vacation. Sometimes there might be a shortage of local parishioners available. Always the senior students were accompanied by parish members, assigned to that ministry of the sick and dying in the local hospital.

Some 'church spy' made a formal complaint to the Archbishop that students had on more than one occasion themselves distributed communion, rather than simply accompanying parish members on their hospital rounds. In fact, I learnt that many of the patients greatly appreciated the visits of the young women from Loreto Mandeville Hall. Never had one of the patients made a complaint about the presence of these senior secondary students or their distribution of Holy Communion.

Resulting from this complaint made by one of the regular parishioners who was unhappy to see this involvement of young people in the ministry to Epworth Hospital, the Archbishop wrote to every parish in the Archdiocese, insisting that only those aged eighteen years should be allowed to assist with the distribution of the Eucharist.

Many of our parishioners felt that it might have been correct with regard to some obscure regulation of Canon Law, but it reflected a real lack of appreciation of the contribution that the students had been making for a long period of time. The young women themselves were not consulted or spoken to by Church authorities. Each of them had, six years previously, received the Sacrament of Confirmation, encouraging them to be witnesses to the gospel.

Serious involvement by young people in the church needs to be encouraged. They will not sustain that involvement unless they are given real responsibility.

The second objection that appears to have been made against the ministry of Fr Peter Kennedy at St Mary's in South Brisbane is that he was prepared to say a prayer or to give a blessing over the committed relationship of a gay or lesbian couple.

This is a clear example of a ministry that seeks to be inclusive within the realms of what is possible within the parameters of the law, both State and Church. There is absolutely no suggestion that at St Mary's, the blessing of such same-sex committed relationships was being equated in any way with the sacrament of marriage. Instead, from what I can understand, the practice of Fr Peter Kennedy was to find some way of acknowledging the value of a committed relationship, for those who had made such a commitment, outside of the limitations that are imposed by Church and State.

Many Catholic priests around Australia today will bless the committed relationship of a mixed-gender couple who perhaps because of a previous marriage are not able to be married within the Catholic Church. This is not to imply that the Church equates their relationship with Christian marriage as defined by church authorities. It is simply acknowledging the value of that commitment with the two individuals concerned.

Most priests have a book of blessings, covering almost anything, from a motor car to a pet! If you can bless a car or a dog, surely it is a good thing to say a prayer over the commitment that two mature adults make to one another, when they are not in a position to share Christian marriage?

Pastorally, couples who cannot marry within the Catholic Church really need some form of support and some acknowledgement of their circumstances, as they attempt to live out the Christian Gospel as best they are able.

Publicly, it would appear that the Catholic Church in many parts of Australia has a great deal of difficulty in finding an appropriate way of providing that form of pastoral care to same-sex attracted people.

In recent years, with the support of most diocesan authorities and the directors of the Catholic Education Office all around Australia, I completed a national consultation report which provided guidance to Catholic Secondary Principals in supporting their school to be more aware of the needs of same-sex attracted students.

There are more than 350 secondary schools which the Catholic Church conducts throughout the country. After the completion of the report, I conducted training workshops for more than 250 of those secondary principals, travelling to all parts of Australia to do so.

In one diocese alone, the report was rejected by the diocesan authorities. It was suggested to me that to use such a report in providing in-service training for Catholic Secondary Principals in that diocese could 'create a situation whereby it is accepted and tolerated that a proportion of our young people do not have a heterosexual orientation'.

Given the high correlation that has been shown to exist between same-sex attraction and youth suicide or serious self-harm, one wonders about the legal fulfilment of the duty of care of diocesan and educational administrators who neglect to deal with this issue or pretend that it really is not there.

Fr Peter Kennedy's willingness to provide a simple blessing for mature couples who are gay or lesbian who have made a commitment to one another is not an uncommon practice for Catholic priests around Australia. He is not alone in undertaking such a practice. What is troublesome is that someone attending services at St Mary's Church in South Brisbane was prepared to formally, but once again secretly, lodge an objection.

The ministry to gay and lesbian Catholics is a fraught area of ministry. It is surprising really, given the large number of Catholic ministers who themselves have a same-sex attraction. One would imagine that it could be an area of pastoral practice where the Catholic Church could act with strength and confidence. Instead, most often it is a taboo topic, one that must remain hidden and unspoken.

The Catholic Catechism urges the church to develop positive pastoral practices with respect to same-sex attracted members: 'The number of men and women who have deep-seated homosexual tendencies is not negligible. They do not choose their homosexual condition; for most of them it is a trial. They must be accepted with respect, compassion, and sensitivity. Every sign of unjust discrimination in their regard should be avoided.' (Paragraph 2358).

It would appear that Fr Peter Kennedy has acted in response to such a directive, as long as the form of his blessing has not suggested that the prayer spoken or the blessing given equated the nature of that committed relationship to that of Christian marriage.

Finally, the third objection that appears to have been made against the community of St Mary's in South Brisbane was the use of inclusive language in the liturgical celebrations conducted there. Again this is yet another example where the local church is being criticised for extending a sense of welcome to those who might otherwise feel marginalised or neglected.

Many church authorities do not understand how important language is, and often church leaders have no idea of how the ordinary person in the pew is affected by language that excludes or demeans. The same could be said for scientists or for lawyers or medical doctors. Often they simply do not appreciate that they cannot be understood, or that what they are communicating is not conveying a positive or clear message.

In the last two decades, many Catholic churches around Australia have become more aware of the importance of language in prayer and liturgical services. Certainly many of the words of liturgical songs have been updated to avoid exclusive language. Many parish churches in Australia have begun to use inclusive translations of the lectionary, in the expectation that the review of the language of the liturgy that had been under way for several years would eventually approve language that while being absolutely faithful to the original texts of scripture would be welcoming to all members of the community.

It came as a great surprise to most, but not all, that the Vatican liturgical commission given the responsibility to investigate this matter recently refused to recommend the use of inclusive language in scriptural verse and in liturgical prayer. There was always the expectation that an inclusive translation used would be scrupulously faithful to the original meaning or intention of those who first composed such verses or prayers.

Fr Peter Kennedy is not alone among Australia Catholic priests who desire to use language in liturgical celebrations that expresses an open welcome to all present, men and women. It comes as a surprise to me that many Catholic Church leaders still do not appear to have any appreciation of the significance of this matter. They do not realise how the continued use of exclusive language affects many men and women in the regular Sunday congregation.

Peter Kennedy's use of inclusive language in liturgical celebrations at St Mary's Church in South Brisbane over recent years is a sign of his commitment to be an effective pastor and to celebrate liturgy that is welcoming to all parties. Who would want a significant part of such a congregation to feel immediately excluded because of the failure of the celebrant or the reader to use inclusive language?

I have limited my comments in this reflection to some observations about the nature of the complaints that were secretly brought forward against the Catholic community of St Mary's Church in South Brisbane. In particular, these complaints were lodged against the pastor, Fr Peter Kennedy.

Each of these three complaints appears to relate to the desire, indeed the commitment, to be inclusive in prayer and in action in the ministry exercised at that local Catholic parish.

If one is bold enough to preach, one is morally bound to preach inclusively. What is overlooked in the discussions about St Mary's, South Brisbane, in recent years is the failing of the Catholic Church to act inclusively. Fr Peter Kennedy's ministry has brought this claim or accusation into the public domain, which is a brave thing to do. Church authorities have responded by laying a counter-claim or accusation, by trying to focus on the failings of the reformer.

How the local church authorities respond to such complaints is never a simple issue to resolve. Others, with more local knowledge, can express their views about how the matter was actually resolved.

All I can express, by way of conclusion, is a great sense of sadness and disappointment at the eventual outcome.

A good priest has been told that he can no longer exercise his ministry of priesthood with the blessing of the Catholic Church.

Those who acted deviously, behind the scenes, lodging complaints to Vatican officials, have been given authority beyond what they deserve. One wonders if they are now rejoicing, or, on the other hand, feeling any sense of regret for the serious damage they have caused.

The local congregation of St Mary's Church in South Brisbane has been divided and, it would appear, largely alienated by the final outcome. Their pastor of many years has been expelled. The community of faith has been dispossessed of the property and the facilities with which they have exercised a ministry of care and support for the poor and the needy over many years.

The priest and the faith community have been convicted and sentenced. What was their offence? Exercising a ministry that spoke of inclusion and welcome, implicitly laying an accusation or criticism of the pastoral and liturgical practice of the wider Catholic Church.

More widely, people from within the Catholic Church and beyond, throughout Australia, and across the world, are asking the question: is this the way things had to be determined? Is this form of resolution one that in any way at all reflects Christian values?

Can the church hear the voice of the reformer or does it feel impelled to protect itself and to turn the accusation back against the messenger?

The voice of the people seems to suggest that there could have been a better way, a way that reflected real engagement and which held out the hope of healing and reconciliation and the continuation of a ministry of welcome and inclusion.

Father Peter Norden is a Vice Chancellor's Fellow at the University of Melbourne, based in the Melbourne Law School. He is also an Adjunct Professor in the School of Global Studies, Social Science and Planning at RMIT University. Peter was the senior Victorian Catholic Prison chaplain from 1985 to 1992, and since that time has been the Policy Director of Catholic Social Services Victoria and the Director and subsequently the Policy Director of Jesuit Social Services. In 2007, he was made an Officer of the Order of Australia 'for services to community development through social research and programs aimed at assisting marginalised young people and offenders, to the mental health sector, and to the Catholic Church'.

PROPHETS WITHOUT HONOUR – MARK 6, 1–6

Notes for a homily given at St Mary's-in-Exile, Sunday 6 July 09

by Dermot Dorgan

In the reading today, Jesus places himself squarely in the tradition of the Old Testament prophets.

A biblical prophet is one who conveys a message from God to a particular time and place. They're not, contrary to popular belief, people who can foresee the future. They are rather people gifted with an ability to see deeply into the present, to look below the surface of society and see the undercurrents and hidden realities that determine what is happening or will happen. The word 'seer' is a good description. An example might be that of a builder coming to your house, your beautiful house with polished floors and newly painted walls and a view of Mt Coot-tha, and saying 'You've got termites in the timbers under your house and the stumps are rotten. It's not going to last. It'll collapse unless you do something'. The builder can foretell the future only because of his ability to see under the surface of the present.

Most of the classical OT prophets lived at a time of prosperity. They saw the corruption and oppression, the manipulation of the poor that had contributed to the wealth and they condemned it in the strongest terms.

And they weren't well received in their own country. We know little of the lives of any of them, apart from Jeremiah, but if the way he was treated was any indication, they had a hard time. Jeremiah was arrested and jailed more than once, he had death threats, he was eventually thrown down a well to get him to shut up, and ended his life in exile.

Jesus saw his rejection as part of that pattern.

This gift of prophecy has always been in the Church. We've heard more about it in recent years, perhaps because it's harder now to keep people quiet than it used to be. People like Martin Luther King, Archbishop Romero, Teilhard de Chardin, Mary MacKillop were all prophetic figures in the same tradition. All of them, by word or by deed, conveyed a message from God to the situation of their day. King and Romero were killed, Teilhard de Chardin was silenced, Mary MacKillop was excommunicated.

The gift of prophecy is found also outside the Church. For me, examples are the environmental movement, the black consciousness movement and the women's movement. These movements told us – tell us – something profoundly true about the human condition or about the unfolding of the universe. And they have also seen a lot of opposition, and still do from some quarters.

I want to mention finally our own community here at St Mary's. I believe it's possible to see our present situation, under the leadership of Peter Kennedy and Terry Fitzpatrick, in the light of this idea and this history. Partly because of the social-justice ministry of Micah projects and the hundreds of other activities supported by this community, which have a prophetic dimension. But also because several of the very things that some people found offensive in our community were, I believe, prophetic actions. People took offence at these things – and it's interesting to note that the Gospel reading today uses the same words for the people's reaction to Jesus.

I think for example that the blessing of gay and lesbian unions is a prophetic act. It results from a determination to look beneath the surface and beneath the conventional derogatory view of homosexuality, and see two human individuals who are worthy of our respect and God's blessing.

I think the presence of the Buddhist statue in the Church was a symbol of the openness in the community to the ways that God might be revealed in other religions and other traditions – and a more general openness to difference.

I think the welcoming of women to present homilies is a similar thing. It's a prophetic act because it recognises the injustice of excluding women from certain areas of ministry and it's an affirmation of their dignity and their equality.

I think that the absence of vestments is an act which cries out for a greater awareness of the priesthood of the laity and a breaking down of the huge gap that has opened up between clergy and laity – a gap which seems absent from the early Christian communities.

Most of all, I think that our seeking to find new ways of speaking about God is a prophetic act. We do this in baptism when we use the words creator, liberator and sustainer of life. It can be seen as a recognition that all the language we use about God has to be metaphorical language. The one thing we know for certain about God is that God is Other, God is different. God does not belong to this universe of which we are a part. And yet the only language we have to speak about God is human language. So when we apply human attributes to God, we're doing so metaphorically. We do this all the time in everyday speech; when we use the word 'tree' for a chart showing the names of our ancestors – a 'family tree' – we're doing so metaphorically. We know that the chart is not really a tree. We can say 'the sea is angry', but we know that the sea cannot experience anger.

So when we say that God is compassionate, wise, merciful etc., we have to recognise that these are essentially human qualities and can only apply to God in a metaphorical sense. God is infinitely bigger than these attributes. So to describe the Second Person of the Trinity as the Son is to use a metaphor, just as it is when we use the word Liberator. In using alternative language, as we do in baptisms, we're trying to explore what it means to say 'Father, Son and Holy Spirit'. And we have to do this with all the language we use about God. What reality are we trying to express when we say 'God is Three, God is One'? What do we mean when we speak about the Incarnation, the Virgin Birth or the Resurrection? We'll only come to a deeper understanding of these realities if we use different language.

We know from ordinary conversation that we sometimes have to say things two or three times in different ways before we can adequately express a feeling or an experience. There must be a million ways to describe the experience of being in love, all of them probably inadequate. But if some authority were to come along and say, 'Look, all this multiplicity of words is downright confusing. From now on, we're going to have one formula for expressing this experience, and here it is – blah blah blah. From now on this is the only orthodox way of expressing this experience. All other expressions are inaccurate and invalid' . . . well, we can see how ridiculous that is. But we're tied to certain fixed expressions of the experience of God, and I believe it is a prophetic act – the act in fact of adult Christians – to look for other ways of expressing our experience.

So all these things we do at St Mary's which have caused such offence to others, can be seen as prophetic acts. And predictably, they have landed us in hot water and resulted in our presence here today in the Trades and Labour Council rooms instead of the old St Mary's building.

And now, we gather here this evening to share in perhaps the most dramatic prophetic act of our Church – the celebration of the Eucharist. The Eucharist can be seen in many ways, and one of them is that it is a great symbolic act in which we look beneath the surface appearance of difference and diversity and disharmony in the world and express our belief in the essential unity of all humanity – by sharing bread and wine. We believe that in this act, God becomes present to us and among us in a new way and with a new intensity and immediacy.

Many of you, like me, may feel uncomfortable here, we may find it unpleasant to be here as outcasts rather than in the church building. But at least we cannot say, after reading today's Gospel, that we weren't warned.

Dermot Dorgan was born and grew up in Ireland. He joined the Columban Fathers on leaving school but after fifteen years left the priesthood and came to Australia. He worked for a variety of organisations, mostly Catholic church ones, in the fields of overseas aid, social–justice education and community development. Most recently he was Coordinator of the Romero Centre for refugees in Brisbane, from which he retired in 2008. He has been writing poetry and songs for the past 25 years and moonlights as a singer and songwriter. He has produced two albums of songs and is working on a third at the moment.

MESSAGE OF HOPE

by Tom Uren

I first became aware of Pope John XXIII soon after he delivered the Easter message of 1963.

Large extracts were recorded in the *New York Times* which I read in the Parliamentary Library at Parliament House, Canberra. I was able to get a copy of the complete statement. I have re-read this many times. I think it is one of the great statements, messages or documents delivered to our human family during the last century.

On April 17th 1963, I asked Prime Minister Robert Menzies a question during Question Time in the House of Representatives in Canberra. Normally, Prime Minister Menzies was a very relaxed, reassured and commanding person. This was the only time I saw him tongue-tied during the eight years I served with Menzies in the 'House'. Regrettably Hansard doesn't reveal his embarrassment on this occasion.

I asked, 'Has the Prime Minister read the text of Pope John's Easter message and if so, does he agree that it is one of the outstanding statements of our time in regard to world peace, disarmament, tolerance and goodwill to all men?

'Will the Prime Minister send a message of congratulations or a letter of appreciation of Pope John on behalf of the Australian Government?'

Menzies looked at me dumbfounded, then asked me if I could repeat the question.

He was still uncomfortable and said, 'I have not been as closely in touch with details in the last few days as I would have wished.

I know His Holiness the Pope issued a message and I am prepared to believe it is a powerful message, because although I am myself a Presbyterian . . . (Eddie Ward injected, 'Yes, a simple one') . . . I happened to be a great admirer of Pope John and his contribution to good sense and wisdom in the world. I look forward to reading the message with considerable interest when the full text of it is received.'

At that time the conservative coalition had very few Catholics in Federal Parliament, the Liberals had Sir John Cramer and the Country Party (Nationals) had no Catholics at all in the House of Representatives. Australian Politics was still a sectarian world; Australia has progressed on that front.

I am not a Catholic but I have evolved in life, I have drawn on men and women of goodwill. My life has been influenced by people like Pope John, Mahatma Gandhi, Nelson Mandela, Martin Luther King and our Mary MacKillop.

Pope John's message of understanding and sanity in the 1960s is so relevant today in our world of conflict and greed, even though the elite of the Catholic Church rarely mention John's leadership. It may have been short, but he has left a powerful message not only for Catholics at the grass roots level but for progressive and compassionate people the world over.

Even though I retired from Parliament nearly 20 years ago, I am an activist and during my life time I have tried to work for the right of the East Timorese for self-determination in their country. Their struggle was not fully understood and there were few friends in the ruling elite, the media, political parties or business.

I served in West Timor in WWII and was taken prisoner of war by the Japanese militarists. In East Timor, no Australians were taken prisoner; they were guided and protected by the East Timorese. During WWII, the Japanese either killed or starved to death at least 50 000 Timorese out of a population of 650 000.

As a member of the Whitlam Cabinet Government of 1972 – 75, I carry a burden of guilt over the Indonesian militarist invasion of December 1975. Since that time, I have campaigned both within and outside of the Labor Party for East Timor's right to self-determination.

East Timor, for many years, was a locked society. Until the Dili massacre of 1991 few people knew what was really going on. That event opened a major public debate particularly in Australia. It was because of the Dili massacre, that I first came in contact with the Josephites, Mary MacKillop's wonderful warriors.

The Catholic Church in Australia was hesitant to become involved with the East Timorese people's struggle. There was a period when it was thought that Fretilin was 'too red'. I have personally witnessed the Catholic Church's change since the Dili massacre. I have been inspired by the Josephites and their allies in the Catholic Church. I have witnessed their influence in the leadership of the Catholic Church under Cardinal Clancy.

I have shared the platform with Cardinal Clancy and I know how genuine his leadership was. He met in Timor with Bishop Belo. I have personally witnessed the influence of the Josephites and their allies at the grass roots level on many other social and human issues.

The remarkable change in attitude to the East Timorese was not only from the Josephites, but from men and women of good-will in other churches and trade unions. In my view it was their enormous surge of support at the grass roots level that encouraged the Howard Government to move so positively in finally supporting a ballot for self-determination of the East Timorese people.

It seems to me without going into the Theology of the Church movements one of the things that touched me so deeply was people like Mary MacKillop and Pope John XXIII. John said in his Easter message of 1963, if you are a Catholic or of another Christian faith or of other faiths, '. . . all should help to develop in others an increasing awareness of their duties, an adventurous and enterprising spirit and the resolution to take the initiative for their own advancement in every field of endeavour. The putting of these principles into effect frequently involves extensive cooperation between Catholics and those Christians who are separated from the apostolic sect. It even involves the cooperation of Catholics with men who may not be Christians but who nevertheless are reasonable men and men of national moral integrity.'

This was a call for people of goodwill to strive for a more just, giving, compassionate world and to protect our planet for the benefit of our human family and other species.

In many ways I have been concerned about our major political parties for their lack of compassion for people and their lack of commitment to the environment – both human-made and our natural environment.

I co-authored, with Martin Flanagan, my last book. Martin's father and I served together on the Burma-Thai Railway. In our book, *The Fight*, I wrote an essay, 'Let Me Turn to the Future', where I drew on my own evolutionary experience and development on issues such as the environment, urban affairs, foreign affairs and defence, to talk in my own way, particularly to our young, about our tomorrow. About compassion, giving and being a servant to our human family. But in trying to communicate this I used substantial extracts from Pope John's Easter message of 1963. I tried to develop John's message of hope as against the hopelessness preached by Samuel Huntington, the Guru of the Necons who argued that the clash of civilisations was inevitable.

What thrilled me more than any other comment was the view of an old Sydney Lefty – Issy Wyner. Issy died when he was 93 years old. Issy was one of the great servers of the people. He was on the Left of the Labor Party but he was greatly loved and respected across the community. He was a former general secretary of the sydney branch of the Painters & Dockers Union, a councillor of the Leichlardt Council and a former mayor.

Issy's 'wake' was held in July 2008 at Balmain Rugby Leagues Club. I attended the wake and during a discussion with Hall Greenland – I knew Issy had been a mentor to Hall – I asked Hall, 'Did Issy think I brought religion into my book by quoting Pope John XXIII too much?' Hall replied spontaneously, 'No!' Issy thought it was terrific. He was so impressed he went and got the full document. It gave me so much joy that this wonderful person with a fertile mind could, in his nineties, be inspired by Pope John. My own personal belief is that Pope John's and Mary MacKillop's giving, servicing and inspiration will continue to inspire men and women to have love and compassion for our human family and for our planet.

Tom Uren is a child of the Great Depression whose politics were forged by his experience of the Burma Railway where he served under Weary Dunlop and saw how engendering a collective spirit saved lives. From 1976 to 1977, Tom Uren was deputy leader of the Australian Labor Party. He was Labor's first environment spokesman, is a long-time activist for world peace and in 1998 was voted a National Living Treasure.

THE FUZZY GREY EDGE

by Susan Connelly

When I was young, I exulted that my Church was 'right', that it was the 'right' religion, and that I belonged to it. We had the 'truth', a position towards which I tried to convince others. I refused to take the Jehovah's Witnesses' publications unless they took my Catholic Truth Society pamphlets; I harangued a poor High Church Anglican girl in the train who happened to make my acquaintance; I made my own posters about state aid to Church schools and put them on telegraph poles. We were right; we had the right doctrines and all the right words.

My father took pains to explain to me about a fuzzy grey edge lying between black and white, but I would have none of it. Now I am amazed at just how wide that fuzzy grey edge is. I had thought it was a cop-out; now I realise it was the space that Jesus occupies. The only 'black and white' realities are a) God is love, and b) the truly human response to a situation or a person must be one of love, and even then it is only God who reads the heart, so one can't judge.

Early in 2009, the parish of St Mary's, South Brisbane, made headlines when accusations were made against it to Rome, compelling the Bishop of the diocese to serve ultimatums which eventuated in the Church building being closed to the community which had worshipped there. It was a tale of secret filming of a Baptism where a different formula was used, claims and counter-claims of a statue of Buddha in the Church, shouts of joyous triumph among ultra-conservative Catholics, sorrow and frustration on the part of the Bishop, the public questioning of formulas of faith by the priest, the willingness of a substantial Catholic community to be sidelined alongside this priest who had served them for a very long time. My one connection with this parish was my complete admiration for it over the East Timor asylum seeker issue in the 1990s. When most Catholic entities in this country were weighing up the advisability of doing anything at all for the beleaguered East Timorese, it was St Mary's, South Brisbane, which took a community decision to provide Sanctuary, symbolising this by joining hands and surrounding their Church building as a human shield.

I have heard of other instances of this parish community fighting for people in difficulty. In doing so the people expressed well the link which Pope John Paul II made between social justice and the Eucharist: 'We cannot delude ourselves: by our mutual love and, in particular, by our concern for those in need we will be recognised as true followers of Christ (cf. Jn 13:35; Mt 25:31–46). This will be the criterion by which the authenticity of our Eucharistic celebrations is judged.'

This extraordinary Papal statement is unequivocal. The standard of judgment of the worth of the celebration of our most holy Sacrament is particularly our concern for the poor.

At around the same time as the South Brisbane debacle, Bishops in the Lefebvrist tradition had their 20-year-old excommunication lifted by Pope Benedict XV1 despite their stated views about the teachings of Vatican II. It was reported on 3 February 2009 that one of the newly restored Bishops, Bernard Tissier de Mallerais, voiced this opinion: 'Asked by the writer Alain Elkann for La Stampa whether the Lefebvrists were thinking of changing their minds on Vatican II reforms, the bishop replied: "No, absolutely not. We are not changing our position, we intend to convert Rome – that is, to bring the Vatican toward our positions."'

On 4 February it was reported: 'Leading Lefebvrists said this week that they still refused to accept Vatican II, which among other reforms condemned anti-Semitism and exonerated the Jews from blame for the Crucifixion of Christ.'

So on the one hand we have a group accused of changing rubrics and questioning the meaning of the words which attempt to express faith realities but who at the same time welcome outcasts, feed the poor and stand up for the oppressed, and on the other we have a group who say all the traditionally accepted faith words and phrases but who publicly oppose the teachings of the Second Vatican Council.

The first group, calling for dialogue, conversation and an episcopal visit, is expelled. The second mouths some sort of apology that the Pope had been embarrassed, and is re-admitted.

In viewing these two wrestling matches I am moved to reflect on the Church, on what it claims and on what it teaches, and in doing so I do not separate institutional Church from the people, because we are all in it together.

A cause for concern is the type of language the Church uses about itself. Its documents describe it with high praise, e.g. it is 'holy', it is 'the spotless spouse of the spotless Lamb'. Its claim to divine establishment enables holiness by association. There is little mention of the other side, the dark side, and when it is mentioned it is usually in relation to individual sinners in the Church, not to any sinful structures, policies and practices. For an establishment which calls individuals to repentance with abundant frequency and consistency, the Catholic Church is very coy in leading by example. How often do we, including Church leaders, admit that we were wrong, or even just mistaken? This lack of balance feeds the mentality that 'we are right, and must always be right'. Nations do it all the time and will probably continue the practice with so little leadership from the single most widely dispersed religion on the planet. How disappointing that despite all the enormous good the Church does, we can just sail on, refusing to look in the mirror. The Church's New Clothes.

It is obvious that our paradigm for understanding the world has changed, because of our greater understanding of the universe, its beginning, its size, its expansion. Any new understanding of our place in the universe has to have a profound effect on our understanding of God, and because of that, of the Church, its teachings and practices. Any attempt to reflect on life as though this new understanding didn't matter is irrational.

The control of the words, the control of language, has been used with varying degrees of success to subdue and change whole peoples, e.g. in Ireland, Poland, Timor-Leste. The loss of language signals the loss of identity, assimilating people into the dominant culture. Language affects thought, hence the Church's reluctance to grapple with God-realities in other than traditional phrases.

The trouble with these words and formulas is that their meaning changes subtly despite all attempts to enshrine them as 'the truth', because life changes people, their language and therefore their thought. Expressions of faith which may have been exciting to the early Christians may now be incomprehensible. Words cannot adequately express mystery. Getting the words 'right' is impossible as they are always limited by time and culture.

So in view of the explosion in our understanding of God as creator of this immense and changing universe, and in the face of a growing militant atheism, what does it mean to say that 'Jesus is God'? In asking this question I am not denying the formula, I am asking what it means in language comprehensible to people, to me, today. What does it mean to say that Jesus founded the Church and that the Pope is infallible in matters of faith and morals when history shows us a deeply flawed Church stumbling in the dark like the rest of humanity? But the Church will not allow these questions to be asked publicly. No pulpit or popular Catholic press would countenance such a discussion.

But there are other questions which never see the light of day either, like 'why can't women be ordained?' or 'why can't priests marry?' Such organisational matters cannot be discussed under pain of being silenced, and the rationale given, in the case of women's ordination at least, is that they are not merely disciplinary, but are the will of God. The refusal to engage with these more minor issues mirrors the refusal to look at the words which express major doctrinal beliefs, a position which either raises Church housekeeping to the level of dogma or reduces cherished beliefs to what is transparently bureaucratic. People can be forgiven for wondering why we are expected to give unquestioning assent to the doctrines when mere disciplinary matters are given the same force, and risk the same Catholic fatwa: that of being silenced if you attempt public discussion.

The Catholic experience in the wake of Vatican Council II can be like the sojourn of the Hebrews in their journey to the promised land, where, in the face of the difficulties of the desert, they pined for the fleshpots of Egypt, food security outweighing the burden of oppression, at least in the rosy glow of memory. We're forty years past the Council, still in the desert, and we don't know how long we'll be here. It is sad to see restorationism in full swing in this Church we love, where nourishment is claimed to reside in the past and nostalgia assumes the status of a virtue. One example is the religious habit.

How much does the current interest in nuns' traditional dress concern the place of women in the Church, the fear of the power of the feminine, the many implications of uniformity? Are religious who don't wear a habit less dedicated to God than those who do? Could the adoption of a religious habit be the answer to the shortage of priests? There are one billion hungry people in the world; what difference will the adoption of medieval dress by some in the Church make to them? Is the fascination with the dress of Church women a distraction from the call of the Council to reclaim Gospel values?

Other questions will be engaging us all in the near future when the new English translation of the Mass is installed. Reasons given for the coming changes include the desire to see that there is the greatest possible fidelity to the Latin text and to give the words an aura of greater religious beauty (in the view of the translators at least). For example, as the response to the oft-used 'The Lord be with you' we will be expected to say 'And with your spirit' instead of the current 'And also with you'. Words rarely used by people nowadays will appear in the prayers, such as 'thwart', 'sullied' and 'gibbet'.

This major revision is not simply about words, but about language, and therefore about identity. It's about what it means to be Catholic today. It's a challenge to me about how I will identify myself within my religion. The attitude which looks to a time-bound text, in this case the Latin, as the standard to which contemporary prayer must be nailed, is no more enlightened than the adherence to the view of the Koran as timeless and divine so beloved of some terrorists. Why is it that a Mass text assembled a mere 500 years ago is translated as though it is beyond cultural and linguistic scrutiny, while the texts of Scripture are brought to us using careful appraisals of the process of their writing?

The Church always has to balance eternity with the time and culture in which it operates. That balance is always a hard-won prize and very often we have missed out. The Church can be too much of this world underneath while mouthing public platitudes about the next. It was wrong about Galileo, and about slavery.

When heresy was a crime against the State, the Church succumbed and conducted the State's police court, the Inquisition. The Church did not speak out against the Nazis strongly enough. The martyred Archbishop Oscar Romero's canonisation was put on hold whilst that of Mgr Escriva, the founder of Opus Dei, was fast-tracked, both decisions being tied up with the politics of Church and State. The Catholic Church in Australia and elsewhere did not give enough clout to its efforts on behalf of the Timorese people, because of political constraints. The Church finds difficulty in negotiating the fuzzy grey edge despite all its claims for itself.

What would it be like to live in a Church where social justice was the norm, where every Parish had a vibrant and challenging group which informed and coordinated the Parish's response to matters which affect the poor and needy, those close at hand and internationally, and where these matters were not seen as belonging merely to the few battlers in the St Vincent de Paul Society? Where Catholic schools put as much emphasis on social analysis as on sport? Where the Catholic press replaced reports of social functions for the well-heeled with free advertising space for those trying to make a difference to the poor? What would it be like to live in a place where politicians listened carefully to the Church's position on abortion and euthanasia because that same Church's stance on all matters affecting the poor was as clear, fearless and unequivocal? Or where the Eucharist was obviously connected to efforts to alleviate homelessness, to addressing drug taking, people trafficking and domestic violence, where Aboriginal persons were invited to come and their stories told and celebrated, where aspects of the liturgy were explained and discussed, their meaning clear and their use accepted as worthy of the work as well as the worship of Jesus?

One thing I can do for the Church is to forgive it. I can say, 'I forgive you, O Church, for your arrogance and hubris. I forgive you for your continued pretence that there is no fuzzy grey edge. Go, and do not sin again.' I want to forgive because for all its backsliding and doubletalk the Church is also my home, a rock of refuge, the cause of greatest challenge, the deepest soul of beauty, fellow-feeling and strength, the school of saints, martyrs and mystics. I want to forgive because I must apply the fuzzy grey edge standard to it too, and not expect too much. The Church falls, but so do I. It makes egregious errors, but so do I. It's the seventy-times-seven scenario for all of us, right throughout life (Mt 18:22).

We do not have the whole story, even though we may think we have. We cannot risk putting all our faith in words, no matter how much hallowed by tradition, as though these can contain the mystery. When it's all boiled down, there is only one Word, and that Word is Jesus. Despite the overwhelming force of both religion and state, he put himself completely into the hands of God, the only Absolute, and identified himself totally with the poor and the outcast. He asks the same of me, and of you.

Susan Connelly is a Sister of St Joseph. Susan has been a teacher and principal in primary schools and has had extensive experience teaching Scripture in state schools. Her association with the people of Timor-Leste has been mainly in the fields of music and literacy, although she became involved in the final years of the people's struggle for independence and that experience led her to commitment to other areas of justice e.g. asylum seekers.

Susan currently works at the Mary MacKillop East Timor Mission supporting the administration of its many activities and initiating various projects.

The support of 65 university students in East Timor is one such project which involves fundraising, administration of fees and oversight of students' progress. Susan is involved in the development of "Hadahur" a Music School in Timor-Leste. She organised the Tour of NSW by a Timorese Choir in 2000, and was responsible for the production of four CDs of Timorese music.

In 2007 Susan was co-author with Margaret Press RSJ of the book Mary MacKillop East Timor 1994-2006.

LAST RITES – THE FINAL MASS AT ST MARY'S CHURCH, SOUTH BRISBANE

by Shane Howard

On Sunday, 19 April 2009, I travelled by plane from Melbourne to Brisbane to attend the final Mass at St Mary's church in South Brisbane. Peter Hudson, a painter whose work I have come to love and admire, met me at the airport. Peter Hudson knew Fr Peter Kennedy well and had great respect for the spiritual and practical work that St Mary's parish was doing. Within a few minutes of arriving at Brisbane airport an announcement came over the public address system, 'Would Mr Shane Howard please come to baggage blues'. Nicole at the baggage counter informed me that my guitar had not made the flight in Melbourne and was on the next flight up. I explained that it might prove a little inconvenient, as I was to be playing and singing at St Mary's church in an hour's time. 'Sometimes these things happen,' said Nicole. She was very apologetic, genuinely.

We raced around to Peter's in-laws and borrowed an acoustic guitar. By the time we got to St Mary's it was 5 minutes to 5 p.m. We entered via the back sacristy door. 'What a beautiful-looking church' was the first thing that struck me from the outside, but from the inside I was struck by the beauty of the woodwork, tile work, architecture. It really is a 'beautiful' building, in every sense of the word.

Peter Hudson introduced me to Fr Peter Kennedy, whom I had never met before. I came with an open mind. The church was filled almost to capacity.

Peter Kennedy had a kindly, passive face and demeanour, but it was not without strength. 'Monastic' was the thought that came to mind.

'Will you sing your song "Murri Time" for us?' he asked.

'I'd be honoured,' I said.

'Murri Time' was a song I had written back in the early 1990s as a love song, of sorts, to my many Murri (Queensland Aboriginal) friends, who despite their many struggles as a dispossessed Indigenous people had always made me feel welcomed. It recalled for me the days I'd spent in Aboriginal friends' homes and in Musgrave Park during many land rights rallies, particularly during the Commonwealth Games in 1982 and through the dark days of racism under the Queensland Act and Joh Bjelke-Petersen's oppressive government. I remember the sadness of singing the song at the old Cherbourg Mission for a young Aboriginal dancer's funeral. He'd died in the back of a police van. Too much injustice. Too much heartache. Too much wrong. It summoned up memories for me of sharing meals and sleeping on mattresses in Aboriginal people's houses from the Gulf of Carpentaria to Kuranda and Cairns and suburban Brisbane. So many people, so poor in material goods but so rich in spirit, despite all the odds.

I was introduced to the choir and the musicians and made to feel welcome. Fr Terry Fitzpatrick led the liturgy. 'All are welcomed, none are turned away.' The altar stood in the middle of the church, in the midst of the community, creating the sense of gathering about the table, as you would at home. Terry was dressed informally with a stole around his neck displaying Aboriginal motifs. It could have felt like a scene from the musical *Godspell* but the voices of little children, the witness of the devout older people and the humbling presence of the poor and homeless kept it all anchored in reality. I was immediately struck by the spirit of the people in the church. As the singing and the liturgy began, I felt that a good spirit was present; that there was a different feeling in that church and community to so many other churches and communities I had been in. At the same time, it was unmistakably a Catholic Mass and gathering. The liturgy was absolutely familiar.

The singing began. Hairs on the back of my neck stood up as the choir and congregation joined in, full voice – not halfheartedly. The hymns and the liturgy were full of meaning and depth. There was a lot more going on than simply repeating words by rote. There was a sense of a deep faith community, committed to the words being spoken, committed to worshipping and acting in the spirit of the Gospels. Aboriginal people, the homeless, professionals, the elderly, gay people, all worshipped together. The community was predominantly and noticeably quite young. The church was full.

The guitar that I had borrowed had no 'pick-up' and couldn't be plugged into the public address system. A young man called Justin stepped forward from the choir and lent me his guitar. In prefacing 'Murri Time', I said, 'The dictionary meaning of the word "catholic" means universal. I and thousands more around the country are inspired by your faithfulness to that notion.' I sang the song and felt moved, deeply moved, in that church, amidst that community.

In his homily, Peter Kennedy, who has been at St Mary's for 28 years, talked about the need 'for more democratic processes to come to the church', for 'the role of women to be expanded' and the need for a 'community of faith'. Celtic crosses adorned the floor and elsewhere. Some sat in chairs, some sat on the floor. Children were welcome and young children wandered. A sculptured cross of intertwining branches was illuminated from the base by hundreds of candles. There was poetry, artistry, social action, faith and justice works. There was meaning.

Halfway through the service, there was a pause and the community began the difficult process of leaving their beloved St Mary's behind for the last time. In silence, with a candle in each of their hands, they filed out onto city streets and began the exodus from orthodoxy to heterodoxy. There were tears. A large Aboriginal flag adorned the front of the church, along with the words 'Treaty Now'. Aunty Malanjalli, an elderly Aboriginal woman in a wheelchair (with oxygen assisting her breathing), led the congregation down Peel Street and, ironically, across Hope Street to the Trades and Labour Council building, the new home of 'St Mary's Catholic community in exile'.

As we walked quietly, Jindu and Waru, two of the kids of my old friend Bart Willoughby, came up to say hello to Uncle Shane. We walked together. I met Michele, a journalist who'd spent quite a bit of time in El Salvador, seeing gross injustice first-hand. She'd seen too much. Seen people being blown up. 'Do you know what a 500-pound bomb can do?' Now a writer, she was trying to make a difference. She said she found solace and meaning at St Mary's since she'd returned home. She said it was hard to find elsewhere.

I also met a sister who had recently left the order, believing the structure and dogma have now prevented the order from being effective in doing the work of the Gospels any more. I quoted Helen Farjeon, who once described nuns as the 'hands of the Gospel'. 'Not anymore,' she said. She had felt bullied and undervalued in the work she had done.

At the TLC building, we ascended in the elevator in small groups and regathered in a large, low-ceilinged, extremely functional office space. We had left behind a place of beauty for an unattractive place of function. But as the numbers regrouped, the feeling we had left at St Mary's rekindled in this new altogether unattractive space. It was apparent that a beautiful building had been left behind, but that was all. The same spirit that had existed in the church was still here in the neutral and unfamiliar surrounds. 'Places are important, but it's the people that make a church,' my father had said to me years ago and his words were in my mind again.

After the service people stayed around talking and drinking cups of tea. When I finally left and said farewell to Fr Kennedy, I asked him what he thought might happen from here. 'They'll probably excommunicate me,' he said. I left there troubled. Later that night he was rushed to hospital with a suspected heart attack. Fortunately, he wasn't admitted.

So what led to this? How did it come to this?

The 'charges' against Fr Kennedy and St Mary's parish were apparently led by 67-year-old Richard Stokes. In a compelling and comprehensive article by Daryl Passmore in Queensland's *Sunday Mail* newspaper in March 2009, Stokes argued, 'My job was to report to the Archbishop in accordance with Church law and, because he did nothing at first, to report to Rome.' 'If you ignore it and let it continue, you allow the evil to continue.'

According to Passmore's article, there are a lot of priests in the greater Brisbane region who know Richard Stokes well and have described him as 'a very divisive, destructive man', with 'a closed mind' who engages in a 'sort of espionage'. Another priest in the region described Stokes as 'the leader of an organised group of self-appointed church vigilantes in the Brisbane region who go from parish to parish, 'reporting what they think is not right to the Vatican'.

Who are these shadowy figures? Is their intent to wind back the reforms of Vatican II? What are their Christian motives? It's hard to see. Will our personal interpretation of being Catholic lead us to the Spanish Inquisition or the Gospels of Jesus?

Passmore goes on to say, 'Stokes acknowledges his involvement in the St Mary's affair is "part of a pattern", starting over 20 years ago when he complained of problems with the liturgy and rubric at a church on the Sunshine Coast. "If I see something wrong, I report it", said Stokes. It would be easier to see this as a small local issue, but Richard Stokes' intervention in agitating and sending video evidence to Archbishop Bathersby and subsequently Rome, broadened the issue to one of much more universal implications.'

According to Passmore, Stokes took issue with the replacement of the words 'I baptise you in the name of the Father and of the Son and of the Holy Spirit' with 'We baptise you in the name of the creator, sustainer and liberator of life'. After he took his complaint to Archbishop Bathersby and was told that the evidence was inconclusive, Stokes filmed a baptism using a mobile phone. Kennedy was infuriated and told him he had no right to film a private baptism without permission. But it's all on YouTube now.

'Frustrated by the slow response of Archbishop Bathersby to his complaint,' Passmore reported, 'Stokes compiled all his evidence on to a CD-Rom and sent five copies to Rome – one to each of the Vatican's Congregation of Bishops, the Congregation of Clergy, the Congregation of the Doctrine of the Faith and the Congregation of the Doctrine for Divine Worship, as well as one to Pope Benedict XVI.'

The Vatican responded and Archbishop Bathersby found himself between a rock and a hard place. It would appear that the wording was what the Vatican took issue with and declared such baptisms invalid. This is allegedly the over-arching reason that Bathersby sacked Kennedy. He attempted to achieve contrition from Kennedy regarding the cessation of the 'improper practices' at St Mary's. Kennedy and the St Mary's community were not prepared to bend and Bathersby decided he could no longer defend his priestly colleague. He was then in the unenviable position of having to offer Kennedy up for sacrifice, due to the protestations of a small rowdy rabble. He ruled that Fr Kennedy had 'caused harm to ecclesiastical communion' and ordered him to leave his role as administrator of the parish. There is a deep sadness in the way that Archbishop Bathersby was painted into such a corner. It would have brought him no joy.

It is the first dismissal of its kind in Australia.

Sadly, this episode is symptomatic of the battle going on for the soul of the Catholic Church and the intransigence and relentless persecution by a handful of doctrinal police has driven a number of people of reason and universal embrace away. But is the Church of Rome really so orthodox as to pursue the sacking of a longstanding priest at the behest of a lay parishioner? Something doesn't add up here. Peter Kennedy is not a revolutionary. He doesn't wish to break away from communion with the Catholic Church. He's simply a good man and a good priest doing good work in a good community, who believes in a broad church and is possibly a little stubborn.

If all the wonderful years of works of St Mary's community can be destroyed by a small group of lay zealots, over a handful of words, then people of compassion, tolerance and forgiveness and liberal thinking should be very concerned. Is there something I'm missing here? I just don't get it, how a priest of 28 years at St Mary's, doing the great work that he and his community do, can just be swept away. It doesn't make sense. Neither does it augur well for an already dwindling clergy and congregation.

Where is the forum for the discussion of conflicting or divergent ideas? Is the Catholic Church really retreating into becoming a conservative cult, obsessed with doctrine over and above the spirit of the word of Jesus? This has happened often enough in Church history and has led to some terrifying consequences. Such were the precursors to the Reformation. Are we really on that slippery slide again or is it simply that the squeaky wheel of dogmatism does get the grease? World Youth Day may have genuinely captured young people's imagination, or it may have been a successful marketing campaign, but for how long will youth remain engaged, before they too retreat from disenchantment with fundamental orthodoxy?

Five days after I attended that last Mass at St Mary's in Brisbane, I read an article about the closure in Buner, Pakistan, of a shrine to the Sufi saint Pir Baba, by Taliban fundamentalists. I couldn't help but connect these two events. They both shout volumes of the rise of fundamentalism in the world of religious authority and a hardening of positions when it seemed that the world was actually moving inexorably towards tolerance, ecumenism and inter-faith dialogue.

The curse of fundamentalism is its appeal to poor thinking and a dumbing down to easy answers. Isn't dogmatism and blind obedience to the letter of the law, rather than the spirit of the holy texts, the same scourge that has given rise to fundamentalism in Islam and Judaism? The brilliant 20th-century Islamic scholar Mohammad Asad wrote, 'The ink of the scholars is more sacred than the blood of the martyrs.' Asad was a Jew who converted to Islam.

Some have argued that the last two Popes have allowed Catholicism to drift back to pre–Vatican II.

In my childhood it was considered a mortal sin to eat meat on Friday. The punishment for a 'mortaller' was hell for eternity. Eating meat on Friday is no longer proscribed, along with many other Church law changes. But what happened to all the people who did eat meat on Fridays before the law changed? Did they ever get out of hell? This is just one example of the kind of contradictory stupidity that arose from the medieval period and remained unchanged for a very long time. An example of church laws that survived from when there was a largely uneducated peasant class. All this changed dramatically in the 20th century and Vatican II was needed to bring the Church up to date with advances in education and reason. Does the Catholic Church still support and endorse Vatican II?

There is no doubt that Fr Kennedy and St Mary's community have pushed the edges of what is acceptable and there is doctrinal responsibility in Archbishop Bathersby's position. Inevitably, though, within the Catholic Church structure it has often been the outcasts and the supposed rebels pushing the boundaries, that have reinvigorated meaning and brought change to the Church. Jesus himself was a questioner and reformer of Judaism. For God's sake, he was put to death for such questioning.

In an article in the magazine *Eureka Street* (27 March 2009), 'St Mary's, Bishop Robinson and the value of dialogue', Fr Frank Brennan outlined his feelings about Archbishop Bathersby and Fr Peter Kennedy, describing them as 'both very pastoral, down to earth, no nonsense men'.

He went on to explain his participation in a public discussion, with other Catholics, regarding Bishop Geoffrey Robinson's book Confronting Power and Sex in the Catholic Church. 'Robinson devoted most of his later years as a bishop to improving the exercise of authority in shaping policies and practices appropriate for dealing with the curse of sexual abuse within the Church.' He goes on to say, 'This is a pastoral book, which does not purport to be a learned theological text.'

'Unsurprisingly Cardinal Pell declined the invitation to speak at the seminar. But he went one step further and prohibited the use of church property for such a discussion.'

Brennan argues, 'The Church cannot thrive when its bishops feel constrained by fear, seeing no need to explain how and why they differ even from one of their own number who is game enough to express dissent from the Vatican's position. In his general acknowledgement of thanks to the unnamed persons who helped him with the book, Robinson writes, "It says much about the need for change that, in the atmosphere that prevails within the church, I would be creating difficulties for them if I gave their names."'

In May 1997 I toured with the Guinness Tour of Irish Music and when the tour concluded in Perth, Australia, I invited the brilliant Irish fiddle player Maire Breathnach to come with me to Broome. She did and when the old Aboriginal women of Broome heard that she was in town they asked her if she would come and play 'Hail Queen of Heaven' for their Novena. Maire could not believe that she was in a remote town, on the other side of the world, attending a Novena with a large gathering of Aboriginal people outdoors, with a statue of Mary under the mango trees in someone's backyard. But there was no denying the reverence and devotion of that novena.

What's my point? Vatican II accepted that there would be regional variations in liturgy. A close reading of the Gospels would surely remind us that Jesus talked of the spirit of the intent in which things are done, not the form.

For me and so many of my contemporaries we were taught a simplistic form of church doctrine. But my generation was one of the first to be educated en masse and as we got older and better educated we began to unravel and then question the hypocrisies we saw. We were inspired when we read Thomas Merton and

Teilhard de Chardin, Sean McDonough, Thomas Berry along with
the Jewish holocaust survivor Victor Frankl. Blind faith was not
enough. We had questions that required answers, but the Church
was mute.

Then we started to have revelations about the extent of sexual
abuse by a small criminal group of priests and Brothers. So many
of my friends are still trying to come to terms with this abuse.
Some have had more than ten years of counselling to try to make
sense of their sexuality and their sense of guilt and shame. One of
my friends was ostracised by his own mother when he raised the
issue of his abuse, because of the perceived shame it brought her
and her family, in the eyes of a church and a community unwilling
to face such a sad reality.

There is evidence that some Bishops knew of such abuse and
just moved the offenders to other parishes where the abusive
and criminal behaviour was likely to continue. Another friend,
the nephew of a well-known and powerful Catholic, suffered
the same fate for bringing shame on the family when he told the
uncomfortable truth about his childhood sexual abuse at the hands
of a priest. Yet another friend had his family ripped apart when,
years later, he found the courage to tell the story of his sexual abuse
by the parish priest who had been in the centre of the family's
life for years. It was inevitably revealed that the priest had a long
history of abuse from parish to parish. Was it not inevitable that
many would lose faith in a hierarchical structure that failed to act
to prevent the sexual abuse of children?

The Catholic Church's response to dealing with such an abuse
of trust has been, frankly, underhanded and secretive. Sacred
trust. For a religion that depends on faith, such a betrayal of trust
undermines the foundation stone of that religion. Jesus had a stern
message for paedophiles: 'Better that a millstone be tied around
their neck and they be thrown into the sea'. A lot of those priests
weren't sacked.

Is there such thing as a cultural Catholic? So many of my
contemporaries were left with nowhere to belong and no church
to believe in. Their only retreat and sustainer was Jesus of the
Gospels. This is not the same as Protestantism, this is failed
Catholicism and many retreated from religion to scripture and/
or culture. Nevertheless, so many of my contemporaries went

out into the world and a large percentage of them have engaged in altruistic work. Social-justice works. But they left the Catholic Church behind. This was a great loss to the Church.

Is this not central to the crisis of faith at the centre of the modern church? The Catholic Church's response to these abuses has been inadequate and it has shamed and diminished the integrity of Catholicism. Adherents of strict doctrine seem to gloss over this crisis of faith as yet another inconvenient truth, but the reality is that the numbers continue to dwindle. A review of causality and policy might just prove productive.

When someone like Fr Peter Kennedy manifests, many of my contemporaries and many of the disenfranchised find that they do have a place to belong as Catholics and a contribution to make and this is reflected in the success of the numbers attending St Mary's and the success of the remarkable justice works of the Micah project. It provides an outlet for goodheartedness, healing and meaningful worship for so many disenchanted and broken Catholics. It also provides a way of bringing those often well-educated 'cultural Catholics' back into active service.

Is it not compatible with a maturity of faith to question the existence of heaven and hell, the historicity of Jesus, the virgin birth, or transubstantiation of the host? I find it hard to believe that any of this would matter to the Jesus who is the subject of the Gospels either. He took on the doctrinal authority of the Jewish Pharisees and high priests of the time and his challenge to Judaism was to live the mystery of God in the world. He challenged them to live in the spirit and not in the letter of the law. Social action combined with worshipful reflection.

The life of Jesus and the concepts that the Gospels advance is a radical one. Jesus did not come to maintain the status quo. His ministry was a challenge to the Jewish authorities of the day who he saw as abusing church law. 'Go and give away all you possess and follow me,' said Jesus, for it's 'harder for a rich man to enter the kingdom of heaven than for a camel to pass through the eye of the needle'. He chased the moneylenders out of the temple. He was no coward and he lived the truth of his belief even unto his own earthly demise.

Here was a Jewish man who was unquestionable on matters of Scripture who astounded people with his knowledge and his advanced arguments, using those Scriptures, to reveal the hypocrisy and self-interest of the religious authorities of the day.

It's all well and good for zealots, all through history, to hide behind the high language that accompanies doctrinal discourse. This is often not the language of the Gospels. Jesus articulated difficult and complex arguments in simple terms, as reported by Matthew, Mark, Luke and John. This is why his philosophical arguments have withstood the test of time and scrutiny. The message is clear and uncomplicated and as such, his story has been embraced and loved by people the world over through two thousand years. Pope John XXIII's biography, from the Vatican website, describes his approach, 'as always characterised by a striving for Gospel simplicity, even amid the most complex diplomatic questions'. On matters of judgement, as Christians, we were raised to believe that we were entitled, even bound, to ask 'What would Jesus do?'

Jesus did not establish a liturgy, a church doctrine, a hierarchical structure, a prescription for what vestments should be worn, what words should be said, other than the Lord's prayer, or a dress code. He did not condone class structure. He said, 'and the greatest of these is love'.

Jesus was a mystic and the mystical revelations in the Gospels elucidate clear and undeniable truths that appeal to us deeply as humans. There are great people within the Catholic Church structure doing extraordinary work. But the hierarchy of the Catholic Church is a human structure, fallible to human foibles, like all religions. History has shown this conclusively and repeatedly. The only truth we have is the Word, the 'logos', and we are left with our frail and flawed human attempts to make sense of such revelation.

In the aforementioned article in *Eureka Street*, Fr Frank Brennan went on to say, 'It is time for dialogue under sponsorship of our bishops . . . the time has long passed for the landowners to deny the peasants an opportunity to reflect conscientiously on the truth and on good pastoral practice. The community roundtables in the national human rights consultation provide a public space where people of wildly divergent views can respectfully speak and be heard. Why can't we provide such spaces in the Church which, as John Paul II said in Veritatis Splendor, "puts herself always and only at the service of conscience"?'

In his homily on the day of that last mass at St Mary's, Fr Peter Kennedy said, 'The Gospels are very powerful narratives. Stories are very important to us as human beings, but stories don't change anything. Stories change people, who then change things.'

The story of Jesus compels us to be good and do good in our lives in the world in the right spirit, not to the letter of a human, corruptible law. Isn't law at the service of the Spirit? Isn't this the inherent narrative beauty and mystery of the Gospels? Aren't we called from worship and reflection to action?

Many communities are having to find new and meaningful ways of congregation. In my own little regional community in south-west Victoria, the local people have rallied, organised and fundraised tirelessly and successfully for over three years, to buy back the church of St Brigid as the focal point for the community. The church was built and paid for by their Irish Famine ancestors. It was closed due to a declining number of priests and parishioners. As a community, the history and legacy of our forebears is cherished and preserved, but the reality is that our community is now made up of devout Catholics, lapsed Catholics, Protestants and atheists. We need each other to be a sustainable community and we focus on what we have in common. The future doesn't exist, it has to be created.

Fr Peter Kennedy and St Mary's 'crime' was to lean toward a modestly different kind of Australian Catholicism. It's not a foreign country. 'All are welcomed, none are turned away.'

'There's a church up on the hill
Some days it's peaceful and still
And the world seems a million miles away
This church that's built of stone
Was made with love and love alone
A light still shines from that church up on the hill'

Shane Howard is a treasured and influential Australian songwriter, both as a solo artist and from his early years as part of the acclaimed band Goanna. His songs have been recorded by artists as diverse as Ireland's Mary Black and Australia's John Farnham and Troy Cassar-Daley. He has devoted much of his working life to working with Aboriginal musicians, as well as touring Ireland and forging Irish-Australian connections. He has worked as music producer for numerous artists, including the Pigram Brothers, Street Warriors, Mary Black and Archie Roach, as well as the Jimmy Chi musical Corrugation Road. He's a recipient of an Australia Council Fellowship, patron of the Spirit of Eureka Committee and a founding member of the Tarerer Gunditj Project Association, a group of Aboriginal and non-Aboriginal people committed to cultural and environmental restoration in Gunditjmara land, southwest Victoria, his beloved home country.

SECOND MEETING

by Martin Flanagan

Our second meeting was six months after the first. By that time Kennedy was slightly more wary of the interview process. After the ABC *Encounter* program did a story on St Mary's, Kennedy obtained the transcripts of the complete interviews they had done with him and Archbishop John Bathersby from the ABC web-site. He listened first to Bathersby and thought what he said was pathetic. Then he listened to what he said and thought it was even more pathetic. It was an Ecclesiastes moment. Vanity, vanity. All is vanity.

Speaking as a journalist, I think Peter Kennedy lost politically. Once they got him and those he calls 'the community' out of the old church that was a Brisbane landmark, he ceased to be news. While they were inside the church, they were news – potentially world news. St Mary's had a treaty with the local Aboriginal people, some of whom used the church as a sanctuary at night. Kennedy says some Aboriginal people had offered to stand with him. He told me the Socialist Alliance also wanted to be part of the action, as did a number of the 'older' members of the congregation – people in their 60s and 70s – grandparents and the like. He gives three reasons for vacating the premises.

The first was that if the church was 'locked down' by the archdiocese – that is, a wire fence was erected around the property on which the church sat – it would also lock down Micah, the social unit started by the St Mary's community. The conflict might also, he thought, compromise the local police. He is full of respect for the local police. 'They admired the work Micah was doing,' he says.

He didn't want to put them in a position where they would have to arrest members of the congregation. His third reason for leaving was that the battle was 'beginning to wear us down'. In that sense, leaving the church has brought him 'freedom and a certain joy'.

But I don't know if winning or losing politically mattered to him. Peter Kennedy is a far more radical thinker than people may realise. The question 'What does being a priest mean?' is not so significant to him as the question 'What does Peter Kennedy mean?' He's now into ideas which more or less obliterate the notion of personal identity in favour of human awareness. He's like a monk steeped in a discipline which is as severe in its way as Zen and is connected to Christian mystics like Meister Eckhart. It owes a good deal to Hinduism and the concept of Advaita. In such a system of belief, the enemy is seeing the world through a divided consciousness which causes us to think in opposites. The aim is awareness and living in the now. 'God?' he declares to me at one point. 'I don't know anything about God!'

He's always been contemplative. When I first interviewed him, he told me how he used to sit, or kneel, in front of the tabernacle. The tabernacle holds the eucharist, the wafer of bread which devout Catholics believe is transmuted into the body of Christ by the Mass. Kennedy would focus on the light on the tabernacle and have feelings of 'peace and joy' which he identified as the presence of Jesus. Now he sees it as an experience of No-thought or No-mind, the object of all meditation, caused by him focusing on the muted light on the golden tabernacle. In terms of Catholic doctrine, there is a world of difference in those two interpretations. Men have been burnt at the stake for less and Kennedy is in no doubt that would have been his fate in another age.

He is, and has always been, a contemplative. He is also a rebel. His case admits to easy interpretation. His earliest childhood memories are of hating his father and loving his mother. Peace was when the family knelt in the evening to say the Rosary. For an Irish Catholic boy from country Queensland in the 1950s with his spiritual inclinations, the priesthood was the closest fit. As a result, he entered one of the most patriarchal institutions on earth, the Roman Catholic Church.

Listening to his story the first time we spoke, I heard about his childhood and school years. The second time I heard more about the six years he spent from 1980 as a priest working in Queensland prisons. He relates again the day a prisoner was bawled out in front of him by a screw. The prisoner wanted to debate with Kennedy a sermon he'd given on forgiveness. 'How can you expect us to forgive?' the prisoner had challenged. 'You know what goes on in here.' When the screw bawled him out the first time, the prisoner said, 'I'm talking to Father Kennedy.' The screw then bawled the prisoner out a second time, saying, 'I don't give a fuck who you're talking to.' Kennedy said and did nothing.

The first time Kennedy told me that story he wept at his powerlessness. The second time I also heard a detail I had previously heard but not noted. At that same moment a white dove that had been sitting on the prison wall flew down and landed on a small square of grass next to where they were standing. 'It may have been chance,' he says. 'But it was a white dove. It wasn't a pigeon.'

He also tells me of the time Archbishop Rush, John Bathersby's predecessor, visited the prison and said Mass. 'He was a decent bloke,' says Kennedy. But he was an Archbishop. He arrived in costume and delivered his sermon as an orator. 'He had this dramatic style.' Telling the story, Kennedy shouts 'Christ! Christ!', like a man who wants his voice to carry to the furthest cell. 'To these men, Christ was a swear word. He (the Archbishop) had no starting point with them. I had no starting point with most of them. He wanted to talk about Jesus sitting in glory at the right hand of the Father in Heaven.'

Kennedy said it was through 'the social Christ, the radical Christ' that he achieved such connections as he made with the prisoners. In 1982, after riots at Boggo Road jail, a prisoner stood up at a meeting and thanked Kennedy for 'standing with us'. 'I didn't know I'd stood with them,' he says, but apparently the authorities did. He started being denied entry to the prisons and, when he got inside and gave the names of the prisoners he wished to see, they might not appear. 'The screws wouldn't call them.'

At some deep level, Kennedy sided with the prisoners against the 'screws'. I noted this because I worked in a prison for two years and did not do so, or not as he did. I was a probation and parole officer. He was a priest. I worked in the prison system. He stood with his flock. It was after Kennedy finished in the prison system that he started reading liberation theology, a mix of Jesus Christ and Karl Marx that took root in Latin America during the 1970s and was an abomination to Pope John Paul II, the man forged by years of opposition to the communist government of Poland.

In July 2009, Kennedy did an ABC radio program in which he was interviewed by six Brisbane high school students. Did he believe in Heaven, he was asked. No, he didn't. Did he believe in Hell? No, he didn't. ('How could a God of love create Hell?' he says to me. 'When Heaven and Hell were conceived as ideas, he says, the earth was thought to be flat. Science has changed all that. If Jesus ascended into Heaven, he's somewhere up in the Milky Way now.') Asked by the students if he believed in God, he replied by saying he had gone to the post office that day. On his way, he had passed a shop with an aquarium in its window with lots of different beautiful-coloured fish which caused him 'awe and wonder'. Feeling he had evaded the question, the presenter of the radio program, an adult, asked him again if he believed in God. 'I've answered that,' he said. He explains himself to me by adding, 'How can you talk about such a mystery in human language?'

He now sees priests and bishops as 'brokers', trying to mediate between people and God. 'The idea is that you can only come to God through them. That's why they need a catechism. They have to have definite answers. You're not allowed to sit with the questions. Who is Jesus? Who is God?' When asked his view on Jesus, he says, 'There could have been a Jesus, but, if there was, he was nothing like the person the Church described over the centuries.'

Judaism, he says, is a religion of dialogue. 'There is no dialogue in the Catholic Church.' He points out that his suspension from priestly duties was imposed without him being brought before any sort of theological court or tribunal to answer the charges made against him. 'What security is there for any Catholic community these ultra-Orthodox people believe to be outside Catholic theology?' Kennedy claims Catholic attendances at Mass are now down to 13 per cent of those who identify in the Census as Catholics. 'Christianity in Australia is dying,' he declares. What about Hillsong? I ask. 'They're not big in the overall picture. Not like the old churches.'

The community he calls St Mary's-in-Exile now operates out of the nearby Trades and Labour Council, although it has had to become St Mary's Ltd and pay taxation. He doesn't know that he'd want to go back to the church if he was invited. St Mary's has acquired some new members precisely because they don't operate out of a church. But there is a fairly simple catch here. The Catholic Church will survive the death of the present Pope. Will St Mary's Ltd survive the death of Peter Kennedy?

There are people who want to nominate Peter Kennedy for a human rights medal. 'I don't want a human-rights medal!' he explodes. 'I don't deserve one.' He's not being modest. He doesn't want a human-rights medal. Why? Because he doesn't deserve one. And, by his standards, he doesn't. 'That sort of mythology gathers around you.' He's right about that, too. Working in the media teaches you that the human need to idealise is in direct proportion to the cynicism and disillusionment which follow in its wake.

When it was put to Peter Kennedy that this book required his name in the title to sell it, he agreed but suggested the following sub-title: 'He's Not the Messiah: He's Just a Very Naughty Boy'. The line, as aficionados of the film will know, is from *The Life of Brian*, a comedy about a man who is mistaken for the Messiah and nothing he says or does can alter the misconception. 'I'm just an ordinary bloke!' he declares. What if Jesus was an ordinary bloke?

ACKNOWLEDGEMENTS

Heartfelt thanks to all contributors whose essays appear in this book. Thank you to Richard Crawley, Morag Fraser, Alan Nichols, Lorraine Gierck, Pat and Vic Wall, Helene Clarke, Tim Kroenert, Andrew Hamilton SJ, James Robertson, Robin Taylor, Gail Pearce, Sean Lehey, Ann Gummow and Matt Walters.

Special thanks to Peter Hudson for the cover portrait of Peter Kennedy.

Also Peter Kennedy, Terry Fitzgerald, Paul Collins, Martin Flanagan, Brian Doyle and Michele Gierck for their kindness and generosity.

A percentage from the proceeds of this book will be returned to St Mary's-in-Exile and Micah Projects.